Stop Narcissistic Behaviors

How to End the Manipulative Cycle with Actionable Advice & Coping Strategies to Recognize Patterns, Find Healing & Build Healthy Relationships—*Even If They Say You Can't*

JORDAN ELLIS

First Printing Edition, 2024
Printed in the United States of America
Available from Amazon.com and other retail outlet

INTRODUCTION

Publishing this book takes guts. It's not easy. But I want my story to be a powerful reminder that change is possible, no matter how deep-rooted your behaviors might seem. I'm here to share with you not just knowledge but my own experience of struggling with and overcoming narcissistic tendencies. This book is born from my personal battle, countless hours of therapy, and a deep commitment to change.

Before we dive in, I need you to do something significant: set aside your ego.

Setting aside your ego means temporarily stepping back from the instinct to defend, justify, or rationalize your behaviors. This isn't about blaming yourself or feeling ashamed; it's about taking an honest look at how your actions have impacted your life and the lives of those around you.

I get it – it requires a level of vulnerability you might not be used to. But here's the thing: real growth happens outside your comfort zone. It's in those moments of discomfort when you're willing to see yourself clearly and acknowledge your flaws, that you open yourself up to genuine self-awareness and the possibility of real change. You might feel a strong urge to resist, to say "That's not me" or "It's not my fault." That's your ego talking, trying to protect you from the pain of self-reflection. But I promise you, the rewards of pushing through that resistance are worth it.

I remember my life before my wake-up call. I was constantly seeking validation from others, always trying to prove my worth through my achievements and success. On the surface, I appeared confident and self-assured, but deep down, I was incredibly insecure. My self-esteem was like a house of cards, easily toppled by the slightest criticism or failure.

It took a particularly tense incident at work, where my defensive reaction to feedback completely damaged my relationships with colleagues, for me to realize the impact of my behavior. After months of working tirelessly on a big project, I was eager to receive praise and admiration from my colleagues. However, when they offered constructive feedback, I became defensive and dismissive, insisting that my way was the best. This behavior created a tense atmosphere and damaged my relationships at work. This moment became a turning point, forcing me to confront uncomfortable truths about myself.

I felt intense shame, guilt, and fear as I confronted these uncomfortable truths.

Through therapy, self-reflection, and a genuine desire to change, I began to understand the roots of my narcissistic tendencies. I started to see how my constant need for validation was exhausting for me and those around me. My lack of empathy and tendency to manipulate situations were creating toxic dynamics in both my personal and professional life. I noticed the hurt on my partner's face during arguments and the gradual distancing of friends who were tired of the drama. I learned that these traits were developed as protective mechanisms. But I also learned that self-critical feelings, as heavy as they are, serve no purpose other than perpetuating dysfunctional cycles.

My journey started long before this realization, and I still work on improving myself every day. I have spent countless hours in therapy, making a huge effort to develop self-awareness. This process has allowed me to see my actions from an outside perspective, feel my emotions more deeply, and put myself in someone else's shoes. I had to learn all of that, and I am a big advocate of the fact that change is possible. We all have things to work on, and it is up to us to make the brave decision to improve ourselves, to become the person we were meant to be.

Everything that happens to us, good and bad, shapes who we are and serves to push us forward on our journey on this planet. Embrace your flaws; they are within you to make you a better person.

The power to change comes from extending compassion to yourself. Narcissistic traits often develop from a fragile self-concept, but they do not represent the sum of who you are. These patterns can be unlearned with vulnerability, courage, and self-awareness.

This book offers the tools and strategies that helped me reshape my life, drawing from everything I have learned from reading, therapy, and personal experience. It is designed to guide you through the process of recognizing and transforming narcissistic behaviors. Whether you have mild narcissistic tendencies or find yourself deeply entrenched in these patterns, this book will provide practical tools and insights to help you on your journey. Let's break down what you're going to get out of it:

First up, we're going to dig deep into understanding narcissism. It's not just about being self-centered - there's a whole spectrum of behaviors and traits. We'll explore different types of narcissism and how they can mess with your relationships. It's like turning on a light in a dark room - suddenly, you'll start seeing patterns you never noticed before.

Next, we're tackling self-awareness. This is where it gets real. We're going to look in the mirror and see ourselves - the good, the bad, and the ugly. It's not about beating yourself up, though. It's about understanding where these behaviors come from. For me, this was a game-changer. Once I understood why I did certain things, it became easier to change them.

Then we're diving into emotional healing. Look, a lot of narcissistic behaviors come from deep-seated pain. We're going to explore ways to heal those old wounds. It's not easy, but man, it's worth it. Imagine feeling whole without needing constant validation from others. That's what we're aiming for.

Building empathy is next on the list. This was tough for me at first. I was so used to seeing everything from my perspective. But learning to understand and connect with others? It's like seeing the world in color for the first time. We'll work on communication skills too - because let's face it, that's where the rubber meets the road in any relationship.

Finally, we're going to talk about creating healthy romantic relationships. This isn't about game-playing or manipulation. It's about building a strong foundation, dealing with challenges head-on, and nurturing real, deep connections.

By sharing my own experiences and the strategies that have helped me, I aim to offer a roadmap for anyone ready to make a change. Trust me. Do not listen to all those people who keep saying that people with narcissistic tendencies are not capable of healing. Yes, it is harder; it requires double the effort, but it is possible. You need a big WHY.

Finding Your Why

Having a powerful "why" is essential as you start this journey. It's going to be your anchor when things get tough. Your "why" is that deep-down, gut-level reason that keeps you pushing forward, even when it feels easier to fall back into old patterns.

We have to dig into this before starting. I want you to sit with these questions. Don't rush your answers. Be honest with yourself - brutally honest if you need to be. It's about uncovering your true motivations.

First, ask yourself: What do I hope to achieve by overcoming these narcissistic tendencies? Maybe it's about building deeper, more authentic relationships. Or perhaps it's about finding a sense of inner peace that doesn't depend on constant external validation. Whatever it is, get specific. Now, imagine how your life and relationships might improve if you succeed on this journey. Picture it in vivid detail. How would your interactions with loved ones change? How might you feel about yourself? What new opportunities might open up for you? Finally, I want you to create a before-and-after picture in your mind. See yourself as you are now, with all your struggles and challenges. Then envision the version of yourself you're working towards. What are the key differences? How does this future move through the world differently?

Take your time with these prompts. Write down your thoughts, even if they're messy or unclear at first. The act of putting pen to paper (or fingers to keyboard) can help clarify your thinking and solidify your commitment.

Remember, your "why" is personal. It's not about living up to someone else's expectations or standards. It's about what truly matters to you. Once you've identified your "why," keep it close. Write it down somewhere you'll see it often. When things get tough - and they will - come back to this. Let it remind you why you started this journey in the first place.

The book follows a consequential order, guiding you step by step through the process of recognizing and healing those emotional wounds that are at the root of your narcissistic traits. I suggest taking each chapter slowly, engaging deeply with the prompts, and allowing yourself the time to truly reflect on your thoughts and experiences. And please, ask for feedback from those who love you! Do not keep limiting your vision to what you presume is the truth because you know what? That is not the truth. It is the reflection of your distorted perception.

Self-awareness is challenging, but with commitment and a willingness to confront the uncomfortable, you can break free from the cycle of destruction. You can learn to relate to others with empathy and authenticity, finding validation and self-worth from within.

Remember, change is a process that requires daily effort and reflection. Remind yourself every day why you decided to embark on this journey. This book will guide you through each stage of this transformative process, offering practical tools and heartfelt encouragement along the way.

Stay patient, be kind to yourself, and celebrate the small victories along the way. You've taken the first courageous step towards a better you; you are reading this book.

One Last Important Note

This book is written specifically for individuals who exhibit light to mild narcissistic traits. As the author, I have never been diagnosed with Narcissistic Personality Disorder (NPD), and this work is not intended to provide advice or treatment for those with a clinical diagnosis of NPD.

If you have been diagnosed with NPD or suspect you may have this condition, it's crucial to seek help from qualified mental health professionals who specialize in personality disorders. The strategies and insights shared in this book, while potentially helpful, are not a substitute for professional medical advice or treatment for NPD.

This book is aimed at those who recognize some narcissistic tendencies in themselves and want to work on personal growth and improving their relationships. It's for those of us who may struggle with issues like seeking excessive validation, difficulty with empathy, or a tendency to prioritize our needs over others, but not to the extent of a full personality disorder.

With that said, for those who are ready to explore and work on narcissistic traits, let's begin this journey of self-discovery and personal growth together.

Welcome to the journey. Let's begin.

PUSHING OUT OF MY COMFORT

Writing a book is tough enough, but when it's about something so personal and you are a narcissistic? That's next level brave.

I've gotta be honest with you - writing this book has been one of the toughest things I've ever done. And now? I'm putting it all out there, asking for feedback. Talk about stepping out of my comfort zone.

But you know what? That's become my life's motto. Push yourself. Grow. Even when it's scary as hell.

So here I am, about to be judged by strangers on Amazon. It's terrifying, but man, I'm proud of how far I've come.

Look, I'm not asking for a free pass here. I want your honest thoughts. But maybe we could start with a little empathy? Baby steps, right?

If you've got feedback, I'm all ears. Shoot me an email at hello@booksquarepublishing. com. I poured my heart into this book, and I want to keep making it better. I really believe it can help people, but I need your input to make that happen.

If you get something out of this book - even if it's just one useful idea - consider leaving a positive review on Amazon. I know you're busy, and it would mean the world to me. Plus, your review could help someone else find their way to this book. It's a small act, but it could make a big difference.

Just click on the QR code below and you'll be directed to the book page on Amazon. It's that easy.

Thanks for taking this journey with me.

J.E.

UNDERSTANDING NARCISSISM

Looking back, I understand how easy it is to feel overwhelmed—and even ashamed—when you first start to recognize narcissistic behaviors in yourself. For a long time, I bought into society's harsh portrayal of narcissism as an unforgivable character flaw. I saw narcissists as hopelessly selfish and incapable of change. I feared that if those traits applied to me, I was simply a bad person, a lost cause.

But I want you to understand this: You are not a monster. You are a complex human being who has developed coping mechanisms and patterns of behavior over years of life experiences—some good, some not so good. Narcissistic tendencies do not represent the entirety of who you are.

The truth is, narcissism is deeply misunderstood. By taking a more nuanced look at what it entails, you start to see these traits not as a fixed part of your identity but as learned thoughts and actions that can be unlearned and reshaped over time. I realized my narcissistic behaviors developed gradually as survival strategies, likely ingrained from difficult early experiences like trauma or neglect. Maybe you depended on excessive admiration to fill an emotional void left by a lack of parental affection. Maybe you prioritized personal success and status out of a desperation to prove your worth.

Once I was able to separate those behaviors from my core self, the path forward became much clearer. You have the power to identify your own problem patterns one by one and decide: Is this who I want to be? If not, you can choose to change it. For me, that meant catching myself whenever I lashed out defensively over minor criticisms and consciously pausing to reflect before reacting. It meant recognizing my limiting beliefs about always needing to be "the best."

I had to get proactive about personal growth through therapy, journaling, meditation, and other self-help practices. And look, this work isn't easy—it takes real commitment to becoming more self-aware and holding yourself accountable. There were absolutely struggles and setbacks along the way. But I kept reminding myself that I'm not inherently flawed or hopeless. We all have areas we need to improve; that's part of being human.

The key is to approach your narcissistic patterns not with brutal self-judgment but with the compassionate determination to understand their roots and actively rewrite those habits. You get to decide who you want to be. While those toxic patterns may have dictated how you showed up in the past, they do not have to define your future. I'm living proof that real, lasting change is possible when you commit to putting in the work. If I can do it, you've got this too.

So, What Is Narcissim?

Alright, let's dive into this. Narcissism—it's a term that gets thrown around a lot, but what does it really mean? I know it might feel like a heavy label, a judgment on your character. But the truth is, narcissism is so much more complex than just being self-absorbed or vain.

Picture narcissism as an iceberg. The part you see above the surface—the grandiosity, the constant need for admiration—that's just the tip. The real substance, the part that can truly help you understand yourself, lies beneath the surface.

At its core, narcissism is a personality trait rooted in a fragile sense of self-worth. It's a constant battle between an inflated sense of importance and a deep-seated fear of not being good enough. This inner tug-of-war is what leads to all those behaviors that might have caused pain to yourself and those around you.

But here's the thing—those behaviors, as hurtful as they may have been, do not define you. They are coping mechanisms, strategies you've developed over time to protect yourself from criticism, rejection, or feelings of inadequacy. Maybe you learned early on that by putting up a front of superiority, you could shield yourself from the pain of not feeling loved or validated.

The roots of narcissism are complex—a tangled web of psychological development, individual experiences, and the influence of the world around us. For some, it might stem from childhood trauma or abuse. For others, it could be a result of inconsistent validation or a deep-seated fear of abandonment.

But no matter where it comes from, the important thing to remember is that you have the power to change. You are not doomed to be defined by your narcissistic traits. You have the capacity for empathy, for growth, for genuine connection—because these are inherent human qualities that exist within all of us.

The journey of confronting narcissism is not an easy one. It requires a willingness to face some tough truths about yourself, to dig deep into those insecurities and past hurts. It takes a lot of self-awareness, motivation, and hard work. But I promise you, it's a journey worth taking.

Think of your narcissistic traits as a suit of armor. Yes, it's protected you in many ways, shielding you from perceived threats and criticisms. But it's also heavy, restrictive, and ultimately isolating. Taking off that armor, piece by piece, can be scary. It leaves you feeling vulnerable and exposed. But it's also freeing. It allows you to move more freely, to connect more deeply with others and with yourself.

So as we move forward together, I want you to remember a few things. First, acknowledging your narcissistic traits is a sign of strength, not weakness. It takes a lot of courage to look at yourself honestly and say, "I want to be better." Second, change is possible. No matter how entrenched these patterns might feel, you have the power to rewrite your story.

And finally, you are not a bad person. You are not a monster. You are a human being, with all the complexities, flaws, and potential that comes with that. Your narcissistic traits are just one part of the multifaceted individual that is you.

But before we go any further, let's take a moment to clear up some common misconceptions about narcissism. It's easy to get caught up in the stereotypes and oversimplifications, but the reality is often more nuanced.

First up, let's tackle the idea that narcissism and self-esteem are the same thing. This couldn't be further from the truth. Self-esteem, when it's healthy, is about having a balanced, realistic view of yourself. It's rooted in self-acceptance, resilience, and the ability to form genuine connections with others. When you have healthy self-esteem, you can acknowledge your strengths and weaknesses, learn from criticism, and maintain a sense of self-worth that isn't dependent on external validation.

Narcissism, on the other hand, is characterized by an inflated sense of self-importance and a constant need for admiration. Sure, narcissists might come across as confident, but scratch beneath the surface and you'll find that this confidence is fragile, easily shattered by the slightest hint of criticism or rejection. It's a house of cards, built on a foundation of insecurity and propped up by the validation of others.

Which brings us to the next misconception—that narcissism is just extreme confidence. Again, not quite. True confidence is marked by humility, by the ability to accept criticism gracefully and learn from it. When you're genuinely confident, you don't need to constantly remind everyone of your accomplishments or belittle others to feel good about yourself.

Narcissistic confidence, in contrast, is defensive and easily threatened. It involves an overestimation of one's abilities and an incessant need for approval. Narcissists often display arrogance and a sense of entitlement, believing they are superior to others. But this superiority complex is not grounded in reality—it's a distortion, a self-perception that requires constant external reinforcement.

Finally, let's address the idea that narcissism is the same as selfishness. While there's certainly overlap, these are distinct concepts. Selfishness refers to prioritizing one's own needs and desires over those of others. We all do this from time to time—it's part of being human. But with selfishness, these are occasional instances, temporary lapses in consideration for others.

Narcissism, however, is pervasive. It's a consistent pattern of behavior that affects every interaction. Narcissists don't just prioritize their own needs—they actively seek admiration and validation to reinforce their self-image, often at the expense of others. They struggle with genuine empathy and may manipulate or exploit others to achieve their goals.

So while selfish behavior can occur in isolated incidents, narcissism is a way of being, a lens through which the narcissist views and interacts with the world.

Understanding these distinctions is crucial as we navigate the complex landscape. It allows us to separate the myth from the reality, to understand narcissism as a multifaceted trait rather than a caricature.

Origins and Definition

The tale of Narcissus is a fascinating starting point for understanding the concept of narcissism. It's a story that has resonated through the ages, a cautionary tale about the dangers of excessive self-love and the importance of maintaining a connection with the world around us.

In the myth, Narcissus is a figure of extraordinary beauty, someone who captures the admiration of all who behold him. But there's a twist—Narcissus is indifferent to this admiration, believing that no one is worthy of his affection. It's a potent symbol of the narcissistic trait of grandiosity, the belief that one is superior to others.

The pivotal moment in the story is when Narcissus catches sight of his own reflection in a pool of water. He becomes enamored with the image, unaware that it's merely a reflection of himself. It's a powerful metaphor for the way narcissism can create a distorted sense of reality, where the narcissist becomes obsessed with an idealized self-image that doesn't match reality.

Narcissus's fixation on his own reflection ultimately consumes him, leading to his tragic demise. It's a stark illustration of how narcissism, when taken to extremes, can be destructive. When we become overly absorbed in our own image, we risk losing touch with the world and people around us.

But the story of Narcissus is just the beginning. Over time, the concept of narcissism has evolved and expanded, becoming a subject of deep psychological study.

In the early 20th century, Sigmund Freud introduced the term "narcissism" into psychological literature. He saw it as a normal stage of human development, a time when an individual's libido, or life force, is focused on themselves. But Freud also recognized that narcissism could become pathological, leading to a range of psychological issues.

As research progressed, the understanding of narcissism became more nuanced. It was no longer seen as simply self-admiration, but as a personality trait with varying degrees and expressions. Researchers identified key characteristics, such as grandiosity, a constant need for admiration, and a lack of empathy. They also recognized that narcissism exists on a spectrum, ranging from healthy self-confidence to the more problematic Narcissistic Personality Disorder (NPD).

In today's society, narcissism has taken on new dimensions. The rise of social media has created a platform where narcissistic behaviors can thrive. The constant pursuit of likes, shares, and positive comments can fuel a preoccupation with self-image and a desire for admiration. The curated highlight reels of our lives that we present online can create a widening gap between the image we project and the reality we live, leading to deeper feelings of inadequacy and insecurity.

Moreover, our culture's emphasis on individualism, achievement, and success can exacerbate narcissistic tendencies. In a world that often equates worth with accomplishments and status, the pressure to excel and be seen as successful can be immense. This environment can make it challenging for individuals to develop a healthy, authentic sense of self-esteem and to cultivate relationships based on mutual respect and understanding.

But amidst these challenges, there is hope. As we become more aware of these dynamics, both on a personal and societal level, we can take steps to counteract their negative impact. We can strive to create environments that value authenticity over perfection, that prioritize genuine connection over superficial interactions. We can work on building a sense of self-worth that is rooted in self-acceptance and resilience rather than external validation.

This is where practices like therapy, self-reflection, and mindfulness can be transformative. By engaging in these practices, we can begin to understand and reshape our narcissistic patterns. We can learn to embrace the complexity of our identities and to cultivate deeper, more authentic connections with ourselves and others.

The story of Narcissus may be ancient, but its lessons are timeless. As we navigate the complexities of narcissism in our modern world, let us remember the importance of maintaining a balance—a balance between self-love and love for others, between the image we project and the reality we live. In this balance, we may find the key to a more fulfilling, connected existence.

The Spectrum of Narcissistic Traits

When it comes to narcissism, it's not a one-size-fits-all situation. It exists on a spectrum, ranging from the occasional self-centered moment that we all have to the far more severe and disruptive Narcissistic Personality Disorder (NPD). The key difference lies in just how much these narcissistic traits impact a person's daily life and relationships.

Let's start at the milder end of things. Here, we're talking about those moments when we might get a little too caught up in ourselves. Maybe you feel a surge of pride when someone compliments your work, or you find yourself eager to share your latest achievement on social media, basking in the likes and positive comments. These experiences are pretty common and generally harmless. After all, who doesn't enjoy a bit of praise now and then? It's perfectly natural to feel proud of what you've accomplished.

The key is balance. If these moments are tempered with genuine interactions and connections with friends and family, then you're likely in a healthy spot. It's when the need for validation and self-focus starts to overshadow other aspects of life that we move into more concerning territory.

As we step into moderate narcissistic traits, the self-centered behavior becomes more pronounced and starts to create some ripples in interpersonal relationships. Imagine someone who is constantly seeking validation, regularly posting on social media fishing for compliments to boost their self-esteem. Or picture a colleague who can't stop talking about their own accomplishments, rarely acknowledging the efforts of their team. They might consistently redirect conversations back to themselves and even manipulate situations to come out looking more successful.

Interacting with someone like this can be downright exhausting. Friends and family might start to feel undervalued, like their own contributions and feelings are being overshadowed. When someone is always exaggerating their own achievements and minimizing those of others, it breeds tension and resentment. Relationships can become strained as people feel increasingly manipulated and unappreciated.

The far end of the spectrum is where we find Narcissistic Personality Disorder (NPD), a more severe and pervasive manifestation of narcissistic traits. NPD is classified as a cluster B personality disorder in the DSM-5, the diagnostic manual used by mental health professionals.

Individuals with NPD display an all-encompassing pattern of grandiosity, a constant need for admiration, and a marked lack of empathy. Their sense of self-worth is exceedingly fragile, tied precariously to external validation. The slightest criticism or perceived failure can send them into an emotional tailspin, their behavior becoming erratic, irrational, and highly dramatic.

It's a volatile and distressing cycle. The individual with NPD is perpetually worried about their image and how others perceive them, leading to chronic anxiety and depression. To maintain this carefully constructed self-image, they often resort to manipulative and exploitative behaviors. They might take credit for others' work, dominate conversations, and dismiss the contributions of those around them.

This can create a toxic atmosphere in both personal and professional settings. Imagine a colleague who consistently undermines their coworkers to make themselves look better, fostering a hostile and mistrustful work environment. Not only does this harm team morale and productivity, but it can also backfire on the individual, damaging their own career prospects in the process.

For someone to be diagnosed with NPD, these narcissistic traits must be significantly impairing their functioning across multiple areas of life. It's not just a matter of the occasional self-centered action, but a pervasive and inflexible pattern of behavior. Often, individuals with NPD lack the self-awareness or motivation to recognize the problematic nature of their actions, making change a daunting prospect.

In contrast, someone with moderate narcissistic traits might exhibit some of these behaviors but not to the same debilitating degree. They may have moments of self-centeredness, but these don't completely derail their functioning or relationships. Importantly, they are usually more aware of these tendencies and open to feedback and change.

Recognizing where you fall on this spectrum is a crucial step in personal growth and maintaining healthy relationships. It's not about labeling yourself or others but about understanding how these traits impact your life and the lives of those around you.

Person With Narcissistic Tendencies

- Exhibits one or a few traits (e.g., believes other should admire them)
- Behaviors come and go, or are only present in some situations (e.g., only at work or school)
- Life and relationships not effected in a major, negative way; traits may even give an advantage (e.g., help them succeed at work)
- May be developmentally normative in childhood and teen years
- Can recognize traits as negative and be open to changing them
- Has/develops self-awareness and insight
- Can be empathetic but may not be at times

Person With Narcissist Personality Disorder

- Traits are fundamental to their personality
- Behaviors are constant across situations
- Traits significantly impair their life, making it impossible for them to have healthy relationships
- Does not see traits as negative and is less likely to be open and willing to work on changing them
- Often lacks self-awareness and insight
- Has little to no ability to empathize; may "weaponizes" empathy and can even be sadistic

THE NARCISSISTIC PERSONALITY INVENTORY

The Narcissistic Personality Inventory (NPI) is a widely used tool for assessing narcissistic traits. It consists of a series of statements that respondents must agree or disagree with, providing a quantifiable measure of narcissism.

Instructions: For each statement, indicate the extent to which you agree or disagree using the following scale:

1. Strongly Disagree
2. Disagree
3. Neutral
4. Agree
5. Strongly Agree

Statements

1. I like to be the center of attention.
2. I have a natural talent for influencing people.
3. I often fantasize about being recognized for my achievements.
4. I believe I am more capable than most people.
5. I feel uncomfortable when I am not the focal point of attention.
6. I can make anyone believe anything I want them to.
7. I think I am a special person.
8. I expect to be treated better than others.
9. I enjoy having authority over others.
10. I am not particularly interested in group achievements.
11. I find it easy to manipulate people.
12. I often envy others' successes.
13. I think I deserve more respect than the average person.
14. I rarely feel remorse for the things I do.
15. I feel I am more important than other people.
16. I find it difficult to empathize with others' problems.
17. I like to show off my accomplishments.
18. I get upset when others don't notice how talented I am.
19. I can talk my way out of anything.
20. I prefer to associate with people who can help me achieve my goals.
21. I am often preoccupied with fantasies of unlimited success and power.
22. I am more capable than others give me credit for.
23. I have a strong need for admiration.
24. I find it easy to exploit others.
25. I often insist on having the best of everything.

THE NARCISSISTIC PERSONALITY INVENTORY

Scoring: To calculate your NPI score, add the points for each statement based on your responses:
- Strongly Disagree: 1 point
- Disagree: 2 points
- Neutral: 3 points
- Agree: 4 points
- Strongly Agree: 5 points

Interpretation: The total score will range between 25 and 125. The higher your score, the stronger the presence of narcissistic traits. Here is a general interpretation guide:

- **25-50:** Low level of narcissistic traits. You exhibit few behaviors associated with narcissism.

- **51-75:** Moderate level of narcissistic traits. You show some narcissistic behaviors, which may occasionally affect your relationships and interactions.

- **76-100:** High level of narcissistic traits. Narcissistic behaviors are likely to be a significant aspect of your personality, impacting your relationships and social interactions.

- **101-125:** Very high level of narcissistic traits. These traits are likely pervasive and may be severely affecting your personal and professional life. It is advisable to seek professional help to address these behaviors.

Reflection and Next Steps: After completing the NPI and reviewing your score, take some time to reflect on the results. Consider the following questions to guide your reflection:

- *What surprised you about your score?*
- *Which statements did you find most accurate or inaccurate in describing you?*
- *How do these narcissistic traits impact your relationships and daily life?*
- *What specific behaviors do you want to change, and how might you go about making those changes?*

Remember, the NPI is a tool for self-awareness, not a diagnostic instrument. If your score indicates a high level of narcissistic traits, consider seeking support from a mental health professional who can help you explore these traits further and develop strategies for personal growth and healthier interactions.

By understanding and reflecting on your narcissistic tendencies, you are taking an IMPORTANT step towards positive change.

Types of Narcissism

Modern psychology distinguishes between four different types of narcissism—grandiose, vulnerable, covert, and malignant. Each type has distinct characteristics and manifests in unique ways, but all share the common thread of a deep-seated need for admiration and a lack of genuine empathy. Let's explore each type in more detail:

Grandiose Narcissism: Grandiose narcissism is often more visible and recognizable due to the overt nature of these behaviors. Individuals with this type of narcissism are typically extroverted and can be charming, using their charisma to gain admiration and influence.

Characteristics: Strong sense of self-importance and confidence.
- They believe they are superior to others and expect special treatment.
- They constantly seek admiration and validation from others.
- They struggle to empathize with others' feelings and needs.
- They are often assertive, dominant, and may come across as arrogant.

Behavioral Examples:
- Bragging about their achievements and abilities.
- Taking credit for others' work and expecting praise.
- Manipulating situations to ensure they remain the center of attention.

Vulnerable Narcissism: Vulnerable narcissism is less overt and more difficult to recognize because individuals with this type often hide their narcissistic traits behind a facade of shyness or insecurity. They may appear modest or humble but are deeply preoccupied with how others perceive them.

Characteristics: Extremely sensitive to criticism and rejection.
- They often feel insecure and have fragile self-esteem.
- They can be defensive and may withdraw or become hostile when they feel threatened.
- They may experience high levels of anxiety and depression.
- They are often more introverted compared to those with grandiose narcissism.

Behavioral Examples:
- Reacting strongly to perceived slights or criticism.
- Avoiding situations where they might feel exposed or judged.
- Seeking reassurance and validation in subtle ways, such as fishing for compliments.

Covert Narcissism: Covert narcissism is particularly insidious because it is masked by seemingly benign behaviors. Individuals with covert narcissism may come across as quiet and unassuming, but their underlying need for admiration and validation drives their interactions.

Characteristics: Have a sense of superiority and entitlement, but they hide it behind a façade of humility or introversion.

- They often express their narcissistic traits through passive-aggressive behavior.
- They may feel resentment towards others who receive attention or success.
- They frequently engage in self-pity and view themselves as victims.
- They use subtle manipulation to get their needs met.

Behavioral Examples:

- Making backhanded compliments or sarcastic remarks.
- Playing the victim to gain sympathy and attention.
- Undermining others' achievements while pretending to be supportive.

Malignant Narcissism: Malignant narcissism is the most dangerous form of narcissism. It combines traits of narcissistic personality disorder with antisocial behaviors, making individuals with this type potentially harmful to others. They are often ruthless in their pursuit of power and control, with little empathy or concern for the consequences of their actions.

Characteristics: Often display antisocial behaviors, such as lying, cheating, and exploiting others.

- They may derive pleasure from hurting others and display aggressive and sadistic tendencies.
- They often exhibit paranoid tendencies, believing others are out to get them.
- They have little to no regard for morality or the well-being of others.
- They are highly manipulative and deceitful.

Behavioral Examples:

- Engaging in criminal or unethical activities.
- Intimidating or bullying others to assert dominance.
- Showing a lack of remorse for their harmful actions.

Recognizing Narcissistic Behaviors

When it comes to understanding narcissism, it's crucial to look at it from different angles. It's like examining a complex puzzle—you need to see all the pieces to truly grasp the big picture. That's why we're going to dive into three distinct aspects of narcissistic traits: behavioral traits, emotional characteristics, and interpersonal dynamics.

1. Behavioral Traits of Narcissism

Let's start with the behavioral side of things. Narcissistic behavior can manifest in a variety of ways, but there are three key traits that stand out: manipulative behavior, an insatiable need for admiration, and a glaring lack of empathy.

Manipulation is a go-to tool for many narcissists. It's how they navigate the world and get what they want. This can involve anything from deceit and flattery to straight-up exploitation. A narcissist might butter someone up with insincere compliments to gain their trust, only to use that connection for their own benefit down the line. To them, relationships are more like transactions—people are resources to be used, not individuals with their own needs and feelings.

Then there's the constant craving for admiration. Narcissists thrive on attention and validation like plants thrive on sunlight. They're always seeking praise and approval to prop up their fragile self-esteem. This can lead to some pretty attention-grabbing behaviors, like incessant bragging, exaggerating their achievements, or even creating dramatic situations where they can swoop in and play the hero. And when that admiration isn't forthcoming? Watch out. They may lash out in anger or withdraw in resentment.

But perhaps the most troubling trait is the profound lack of empathy. Narcissists often struggle to understand and connect with the emotions of others. They're so focused on their own needs and desires that they find it difficult to be genuinely compassionate or supportive. This can lead to some incredibly insensitive and hurtful behaviors. A narcissist might dismiss a friend's concerns as trivial or unimportant, too wrapped up in their own issues to offer any real comfort.

How to Stop Being the Center of Attention. Learning to step out of the spotlight isn't about becoming invisible or denying your own worth. It's about finding a balance, about recognizing that everyone has value and something to contribute. It takes practice, and there are days when I still slip up. But the relationships I've built, the connections I've made since I started doing this and deeper and more genuine than anything I had before.

First up, let's talk about active listening. Man, I used to be terrible at this. I'd hear someone talking and immediately start thinking about what I was going to say next, or how I could turn the conversation back to me. Now, I try to really listen. Like, actually pay attention to what they're saying. Ask questions. Show that I'm interested. It's amazing how much you can learn when you shut up and listen.

In group settings, I've had to learn to share the stage. This was tough at first. I was used to dominating conversations, making sure everyone knew how smart or funny or successful I was. Now, I make a conscious effort to let others speak. I even try to draw out the quieter folks. Turns out, they often have the most interesting things to say!

Celebrating others is a huge one. Instead of always talking about my your achievements, try to recognize what others are doing. Giving a genuine compliment feels good, and it helps take the focus off you.

So give it a shot. Try taking a step back, letting others shine. You might be surprised at how good it feels to not always be in the spotlight.

Recognizing and Avoiding Manipulation. Manipulation is not always as obvious as we think. Sometimes it's subtle stuff like guilt-tripping or playing the victim. I used to do this thing where I'd make people feel bad for not giving me what I wanted. It worked, sure, but it left me feeling like crap and made my relationships toxic.

Avoiding manipulation is all about choosing the high road, even when it's not the easiest path. It's about being straight up with people, even when you're tempted to twist things to your advantage. Before you interact with someone, take a second to check your intentions. Are you genuinely trying to connect, or are you trying to get something out of them? It's not always easy to be honest with yourself, but it's crucial.

Respecting boundaries is another big one. I used to see other people's boundaries as challenges to overcome. If someone said no, I'd try to find a way around it. Now, I get it. No means no. If a friend tells me they're too busy to hang out, I don't guilt-trip them or try to change their mind. I respect their time and their decision.

Manipulation might get you what you want in the short term, but it erodes trust and damages relationships in the long run. Being honest and respecting boundaries? That builds trust.

Start small. Maybe next time you're tempted to manipulate a situation, pause and ask yourself if there's a more honest way to handle it

2. Emotional Characteristics of Narcissism

Moving on to the emotional realm, the inner world of a narcissist can be a rollercoaster. There are some key emotional characteristics to be aware of, including superiority, instability, and an intense sensitivity to criticism.

Narcissists often harbor an unshakable belief in their own superiority. They see themselves as better, smarter, and more deserving than everyone else. This sense of superiority can manifest as arrogance and a dismissive attitude towards those they deem inferior. Imagine a narcissist in a work meeting, belittling a colleague's ideas not because they're bad ideas, but because they believe their own ideas are inherently better. It's a surefire way to alienate others and create conflict.

Despite the outward bravado, narcissists often grapple with significant emotional instability. Their self-esteem is fragile, and their mood can pivot dramatically based on the external validation or criticism they receive. Praise can send them soaring to euphoric heights, but criticism or failure can plunge them swiftly into anxiety, anger, or depression. It's a volatile emotional landscape that can make relationships with narcissists particularly challenging for those around them.

And then there's the extreme sensitivity to criticism. Even the most minor or constructive feedback can feel like a scathing personal attack to a narcissist. They often react with intense defensiveness, either lashing out in anger or retreating into denial. Imagine a supervisor pointing out a mistake to a narcissistic employee. Rather than taking the feedback on board, they might react with rage, blame others, or even try to undermine the supervisor to protect their own sense of superiority. This sensitivity can be a major roadblock to personal growth.

How to Cope with Criticism. I used to feel like every bit of feedback was a personal attack. But here's the thing I've learned: criticism doesn't have to be your enemy. It can actually be a tool for growth if you know how to handle it. So let me share some strategies that have helped me, and maybe they can help you too.

When someone's giving you feedback, I know your first instinct might be to jump in and defend yourself, instead pause for a second. Take a deep breath....it's amazing how much clearer you can think with just that small pause! Really listen to what they're saying. Don't just wait for your turn to talk. Try to understand where they're coming from.

You are not under attack. The criticism isn't about YOU as a person. It's about something you did or said. Your worth isn't on the line here. I used to feel like any criticism meant I was a failure, but that's not true. We all make mistakes, we all have room to improve and we all have different opinions anyway.

If you're not sure what they mean, ask. It's okay to say, "Can you give me an example?" or "What would you suggest I do differently?" This isn't admitting defeat - it's gathering information.

After the conversation, take some time to think about what was said. Is there any truth to it? Even if you don't agree with everything, there might be something you can learn. I've found some of my biggest improvements came from feedback I initially didn't want to hear Learning to handle criticism is about using it to become the best version of yourself. And the growth you'll see in yourself? It's worth every uncomfortable moment.

How to Practice Humility. The idea of being humble can feel like we're giving up our power. I used to think admitting I wasn't perfect at everything was a sign of weakness. But you know what? It's actually liberating. It takes the pressure off trying to be super-human all the time.

Humility isn't about thinking less of yourself. It's about thinking of yourself less. It's about recognizing that you're part of something bigger than just you. It is like a reality check. It grounds you. It helps you see the world more clearly, not just through the lens of your own ego.

I've got some strategies that have really helped me. Maybe they'll work for you too.

1. Really listen to other people....You'd be amazed at what you can learn when you shut up and pay attention. It's humbling to realize how much wisdom other people have to offer.

2. Own your mistakes. When you screw up, admit it. No excuses, no deflecting blame. Just a simple, "I messed up, and I'm sorry." It feels vulnerable as hell at first, but it actually makes you look stronger, not weaker.

3. Try celebrating other people's wins. I know, when someone else succeeds, it can feel like it takes something away from you. But flip that script. Their success doesn't diminish you. Cheering for others can actually make you feel pretty good.

4. Gratitude is huge. Take time each day to appreciate what you have and the people in your life. It's hard to feel superior when you're busy feeling thankful.

5. Self-reflection is key. Take a hard look at your behavior. How are you impacting the people around you? Are you living up to your own values? It's not always comfortable, but it's how we grow.

6. Get out there and help someone. Volunteer, do a favor for a friend, whatever. When you're focused on serving others, it's hard to stay self-centered.

7. Lastly, ask for feedback. Yeah, it's scary. But ask people you trust to be honest about how you're doing. And here's the hard part - really listen to what they say.

3. Interpersonal Dynamics of Narcissism

Finally, let's look at how narcissism plays out in interpersonal dynamics across various contexts—family, friends, and the workplace. By examining these different areas, we can get a more comprehensive understanding of the pervasive impact of narcissism.

In relationships, narcissists often fall into patterns of control and dominance. They might start out all charm and charisma, drawing people in with their confidence. But as the relationship progresses, they can become increasingly controlling and demanding, expecting constant admiration and compliance. It's a cycle of idealization, devaluation, and discard—they build someone up, then tear them down, and ultimately cast them aside when they no longer serve their needs.

The impact on family and friends can be particularly damaging. In family settings, narcissists may manipulate relatives, playing them against each other to remain the center of attention or to avoid blame. For friends, the constant need for validation and the narcissist's inability to provide genuine support can be exhausting. Imagine a narcissist constantly demanding that a friend cancel their plans to cater to their needs, with little regard for the friend's own life and feelings. Over time, this one-sided dynamic can lead to strained or broken relationships as people pull away to protect their own well-being.

In the workplace, narcissistic behavior can be a major disruptor to team dynamics and productivity. Narcissists often seek out positions of power and may undermine colleagues to get ahead. Their insatiable need for admiration can drive them to take credit for others' work or exaggerate their own contributions. This can foster a toxic work environment rife with competition, mistrust, and conflict, leaving colleagues feeling demoralized and undervalued.

Picture a narcissistic manager who routinely takes credit for the team's successes but is quick to blame team members for any failures. This erosion of trust and cooperation can severely impact team morale and productivity, as employees become increasingly wary and fearful of making mistakes.

How to Let Go of Control. I used to think I had to have my fingers in every pie, you know? If I wasn't calling the shots, I felt like everything would fall apart.

First things first, we've got to recognize what sets us off. For me, it was anytime I felt uncertain or vulnerable. I'd start micromanaging everything and everyone around me. Figuring out these triggers was like finding the key to a lock I didn't even know was there.

Accepting uncertainty is key here. I wanted to plan for every possibility, control every outcome. But life doesn't work that way. Learning to roll with the punches, to accept that sometimes things are out of my hands? It's part of the journey.

I had to learn to delegate. That was tough. I mean, nobody could do things as well as I could, right? Wrong. I started small, letting others handle minor tasks. And you know what? The world didn't end. In fact, sometimes they did a better job than I would have. Next time you feel that urge to control everything, ask yourself if you really need to be in charge of the situation. You might be surprised at how good it feels to just let things unfold sometimes.

How to Stop Compulsive Lying. I used to lie about big things, small things, anything to make myself look better or avoid uncomfortable situations...it might feel like a quick fix, but it's poison to your relationships and your self-respect.

First step? I had to start paying attention to when and why I was lying. It was eye-opening, and honestly, a bit embarrassing. I'd lie about my accomplishments to impress people, or make up excuses to avoid commitments. Just being aware of it was a huge step.

Then came the hard part - figuring out why I felt the need to lie. Was I that insecure? Was I afraid of letting people see the real me?

Making the decision to be honest, even when it's uncomfortable, that's where the rubber meets the road. I started small. If someone asked how I was doing, I'd give an honest answer instead of the automatic "I'm fine." It felt weird at first, but also... freeing, again.

Finding someone to keep me accountable was crucial. I told my best friend about my struggle and asked him to call me out if he caught me in a lie. It was humbling, but having that support made a big difference.

Look, Tthere are still times when I feel that old urge to embellish the truth or avoid responsibility. But every time I choose honesty, even when it's hard, I feel a little bit stronger, a little more authentic. People trust me more. And I can look at myself in the mirror without feeling like a fraud.

THE ROAD TO SELF-AWARENESS

Admitting you have narcissistic traits is often the hardest step but also the most crucial for real change. I know—it was excruciating for me to finally confront that harsh reality about myself. It takes raw honesty, bravery, and a willingness to look your flaws square in the eye.

I get it—vulnerability requires confronting painful emotions and admitting you're imperfect, which can feel absolutely terrifying when your self-worth is so fragile. That fear often translates into flat-out rejecting or rationalizing away any feedback that bruises the ego.

But here's the thing: As daunting as it is, you can overcome those defensive behaviors with true dedication and the right support system.

Having a skilled therapist create that safe, judgment-free zone to explore the depth of your narcissistic tendencies is huge. Mindfulness practices like meditation allow you to objectively observe your thoughts and emotions, so you can identify the root insecurities and triggers Something as simple as journaling your thoughts, feelings, and reactions can reveal eye-opening patterns you may have been blind to before. When you have people in your life you trust, being open to their perspective can challenge narcissistic thinking in a way you can't do alone.

At the end of the day, though, the biggest obstacle is that fear of being vulnerable. Allowing yourself to feel and express emotions honestly, acknowledging fears and flaws—that's where the real strength lies. It's a journey for sure, but every ounce of vulnerability and honest self-awareness plants you one step closer to positive, lasting change.

Don't retreat back, have courage to keep exploring because breaking free is absolutely possible. Take a moment to reflect on these questions—and be brutally honest with yourself:

1. *Do you constantly crave praise and validation from others? When you don't get the reassurance you feel you deserve, does it leave you feeling upset or unappreciated?*

2. *How do you typically react when someone critiques you? Does your immediate response involve lashing out defensively because, deep down, it feels like an attack on your self-worth?*

3.

4. *Be real—do you low-key believe you should get special privileges or treatment that others don't? When things don't go your way, do you get instantly frustrated because you're used to calling the shots?*

5. *This is a tough one, but try to look inward: Do you ever actually make an effort to understand how someone else is feeling in a given situation? Or do you just dismiss their emotions because your perspective is the only one that really matters?*

6. *Have you developed tactics to manipulate people into giving you what you want, like lying, exaggerating, laying on guilt trips, or flattery?*

7. *Honestly ask yourself—do you have a tendency to look down on others, feeling a sense of superiority because you see them as less capable or intelligent than you?*

8. *When something goes wrong, are you able to own your role in the consequences? Or does blame-shifting and making excuses feel like an automatic defensive reflex?*

Real growth happens when you can look at yourself with unfiltered honesty. If any of those hit a little too close to home, don't run from it. Lean into that discomfort—that's how you start dismantling the narcissistic behaviors, bit by bit.

Understanding Your Behaviors and Their Origins

The environments we grow up in, especially the dynamics within our families, leave a profound imprint on our personalities and the coping mechanisms we develop—for better or worse. We'll delve deeper into this topic later, but it's worth touching on briefly here.

Think back to your childhood household and the vibe between you and your parents or caregivers. Those earliest interactions play a huge role in shaping your attachment styles—how you learned to relate to others and what you came to expect from relationships. If you felt securely attached, it likely fostered a solid sense of trust. But if that attachment was more insecure or strained, it can breed anxiety around intimacy and a tendency to be avoidant or ambivalent with others. Maybe you developed that gnawing need for constant validation or struggle to open up because trust issues run deep.

Within families, people often naturally fall into roles too. Maybe you were the high-achiever, always hustling for accolades and parental approval, or the rebellious troublemaker who acted out for attention. Those boxes we get put in at a young age, whether by parents or siblings, can create distorted self-perceptions that breed narcissistic behavioral patterns down the road.

Then there are the parenting styles themselves to consider. Were your parents the strict disciplinarian type? Or were boundaries pretty lax and there wasn't much authority? Those authoritarian or permissive approaches can both breed narcissistic traits in different ways—like having issues with authority figures, shaky self-esteem, or underdeveloped social skills. An authoritative parenting style that balances nurturance with discipline tends to lead to healthier emotional outcomes.

The emotional support and validation (or lack thereof) you got from your parents is key too. Consistent emotional attunement from caregivers helps kids develop self-worth and learn to regulate their emotions in a healthy way. But when that's missing, it can leave you internalizing: "I'm not good enough" or "my feelings don't matter." And let's be real—if your parents modeled crappy behavior like aggression, dishonesty, or just weren't present emotionally, those became the examples you learned from whether you realized it or not.

So while unpacking all the childhood stuff can feel heavy and complicated, the reality is those early experiences and family dynamics shaped so many of our fundamental beliefs and behavior patterns. Self-awareness is half the battle in breaking the cycles.

Having a Parent with Narcissistic Traits

Growing up with a narcissistic parent really does a number on you. I remember constantly walking on eggshells, never knowing if I'd be showered with praise one minute or torn down the next. It was like living in an emotional minefield. My old man, he was all about himself. His needs, his ego—that's what our family revolved around. And me? I learned pretty quickly that my job was to make him look good, to be his little trophy. My own feelings? They didn't matter much. It's the kind of upbringing that really shapes your whole perspective in an incredibly painful way.

I can still hear his voice in my head sometimes, you know? That constant criticism, always pushing me to be "better"—which really meant being what he wanted me to be. It messed me up for a long time. I'd second-guess every decision, always wondering if I was good enough. And relationships? Don't get me started. For the longest time, I either clung to people, desperate for any scrap of approval, or I'd push them away before they could reject me. It was like I didn't know how to just... be normal with people.

It took me years to realize that this wasn't just "tough love" or "high standards." This was straight-up emotional neglect. And that realization hurt like hell, but it was also the start of my healing. I had to learn how to parent myself, in a way. To give myself the love and validation I never got as a kid. It's been a long road, lots of therapy, lots of hard looks in the mirror. But I'm definitely getting there.

If you're in the same boat, if you're dealing with the aftermath of a narcissistic parent, I want you to know—it's not your fault. You deserved better. And it's never too late to start healing. It's no easy road, but you've got this. That vital spark of motivation, refusing to let your story endlessly repeat those toxic cycles—that's how you reclaim your identity and cultivate the self-love you deserved from the start.

Journaling Prompts: The goal with these isn't to dwell in misery but to build honest self-awareness. Once you can shine light on those wounds and unhealed patterns, you open the door to real growth and self-compassion. It's all part of the journey.

1. *Think back to specific memories or situations with your parents that made you feel ma-nipulated, criticized, or neglected as a kid. What was going through your mind, and how did it make you feel in those moments? See if you can revisit those painful emotions without judgment.*

2. *In your current adult relationships, do any behavior patterns ring familiarly from child-hood—like the need to constantly please others out of fear they'll reject or abandon you? How might those insecurities rooted in the past be influencing your connections today?*

3. *Get honest with yourself about the emotional support (or lack thereof) you felt from your parents. Were there times you can remember feeling really seen, understood, and validated by them? Or did you constantly feel dismissed and that your feelings didn't matter? How has that shaped your own self-worth over time?*

4. *Recall a specific situation where you shoved down your own needs or emotions as a kid because expressing them felt unsafe or like it would jeopardize getting your parents' ap-proval and affection. Look at how having to repress your authentic self back then may still be playing out in your adult behaviors and thought patterns.*

5. *Empathy is such a crucial ingredient for emotional attunement. Reflect on how em-pathetic (or not) your parents were in relating to your inner experiences and reading emotional cues. How did their level of empathy impact your own ability to form deep, emotionally-attuned bonds later in life?*

Childhood Trauma and Its Long-Term Effects

For those raised by a narcissistic parent or who endured other forms of childhood trau-ma, the impacts on emotional health, behavior patterns, and cognitive processes can be tremendously damaging. Trauma of any kind during those formative years gets hard-wired into our psyches in insidious ways:

- **Emotional Impact:** Childhood trauma can lead to difficulties in emotional regula-tion, increased anxiety, depression, and a heightened stress response. Traumatized children may struggle with feelings of worthlessness, guilt, and chronic fear.

- **Behavioral Consequences:** Trauma can also result in behavioral issues, such as ag-gression, withdrawal, or difficulties in forming healthy relationships. These behav-iors often serve as coping mechanisms to deal with the unresolved pain and fear stemming from traumatic experiences.

- **Cognitive Distortions:** Trauma can alter cognitive processes, leading to distorted thinking patterns such as catastrophizing, black-and-white thinking, or excessive self-blame. These distortions can persist into adulthood, affecting decision-making and interpersonal relationships.

I know this firsthand from my own turbulent upbringing. My father exhibited classic narcissistic behaviors—he constantly sought admiration, easily felt slighted, and dismissed my feelings with cruel indifference whenever I dared to be vulnerable around him. As a child, having your emotional world diminished in that way sends such a distorted, damaging message about your worth. Not surprisingly, I quickly learned to suppress my authentic thoughts and emotions as a way to avoid triggering his outbursts or cold disapproval. Instead, I became a prime people-pleaser who twisted myself into knots seeking his validation and approval at all costs. This unhealthy dynamic fostered deep insecurities, fears of abandonment, and skewed ideas about intimacy that spilled into my adult relationships.

For children raised in such an environment, the tendency to develop narcissistic defense mechanisms like denial, entitlement, and lack of empathy makes perfect sense. These coping methods, however maladaptive in the long run, initially arise as self-preservation tactics to guard against future emotional neglect or abuse.

The good news is, with insight and intentional work, it's absolutely possible to dismantle these long-standing patterns, even those rooted in childhood experiences. Unpacking the "why" behind narcissistic behaviors through journaling, therapy, or self-reflection starts to relieve their grip. And over time, you can rewrite the narratives that kept those toxic cycles spinning.

Overcoming Denial

We all have a tendency to slip into denial at times—it's one of the mind's default defense mechanisms for avoiding those uncomfortable truths about ourselves. I get it; denial can feel like a necessary shield, allowing you to maintain some sense of control and superiority rather than confront vulnerabilities head-on.

But here's the hard reality—that protective shell of denial ultimately comes at a massive cost. It straight up prevents you from addressing the harmful behaviors and blind spots that are sabotaging your closest relationships.

I know I've certainly been guilty of denial playing out in toxic ways, like constantly interrupting my partner because I arrogantly believed my thoughts and perspectives were just more important than theirs. That denial allowed me to justify those self-centered tendencies rather than realize how unheard and devalued I was making them feel.

Or I'd dismiss friends who had the courage to call out my narcissistic behavior, just writing them off as overreacting rather than taking an honest look inward. Obviously, that denial created resentment and distance in those bonds.

The uncomfortable truth is that denial morphs into all sorts of ugly forms when narcissistic traits are involved. But, for the purpose of our book, we will focus on the three main mechanisms that are particularly relevant—I know them all too well, they were my go-to strategies for years, and they did a number on me and my relationships.

Projection: Projection involves attributing one's own unacceptable thoughts or feelings to someone else. It serves as a way to deflect responsibility and avoid facing their own flaws.

Imagine a person named Alex who constantly accuses his partner, Jamie, of being needy and craving attention. In reality, Alex is the one who requires constant validation and attention. By projecting his insecurities onto Jamie, Alex avoids acknowledging his own dependency issues.

Strategies to Overcome Projection:

Self-Reflection:
- Spend a few minutes each day reflecting on your thoughts and feelings without judgment. Notice when you feel the urge to project onto others.
- Write about moments when you felt the need to blame others. Ask yourself, "Could this be something I'm struggling with myself?"

Seek Feedback:
- Request honest feedback about your behavior and listen without getting defensive.
- Work with a therapist to identify patterns of projection and develop healthier ways to address your own insecurities.

Accountability Partners:
- Have a friend or family member help you recognize when you're projecting.
- Discuss situations where projection might occur and strategies to handle them differently.

Rationalization: Rationalization involves creating logical but false explanations for behaviors driven by unacceptable impulses. We use rationalization to justify our actions and avoid confronting their true motivations.

Consider Sara, who frequently belittles her colleagues' ideas in meetings. She rationalizes this behavior by convincing herself that she is just trying to maintain high standards and push the team to excel, rather than admitting that she feels threatened by their competence.

Strategies to Overcome Rationalization:

Challenge Your Beliefs:
- When you find yourself rationalizing, question the validity of your reasoning. Ask, "Is this really true, or am I trying to justify my behavior?"
- Look for factual evidence that either supports or refutes your rationalizations.

Practice Honesty:
- Acknowledge when you are making excuses rather than addressing the real issue.
- Admit when you've made a mistake or acted out of insecurity.

Focus on Empathy:
- Try to understand how your actions affect others. Ask yourself, "How would I feel if I were in their shoes?"

- Instead of justifying your actions, have open discussions about your intentions and be willing to accept constructive criticism.

Minimization: Minimization involves downplaying the severity or impact of a behavior or situation. Narcissistic individuals might acknowledge a problem but insist that it is not as serious as others make it out to be.

Imagine John, who occasionally insults his partner during arguments. When confronted, he minimizes the impact by saying, "I was just joking, you're too sensitive," instead of recognizing the hurtful nature of his words.

Strategies to Overcome Minimization:

Acknowledge Feelings:
- Accept that others' feelings are valid and important, even if you don't fully understand them.
- Make an effort to empathize with others' experiences and recognize the impact of your actions.

Increase Self-Awareness:
- Document instances where you might be minimizing situations. Reflect on the real impact of your actions.
- Talk to a therapist or trusted friend who can provide an unbiased view of your behavior.

Accept Responsibility:
- Acknowledge when you've caused harm and take it seriously, regardless of your initial perception.
- Take steps to repair the damage caused by your actions, showing that you understand the significance of the issue.

Overcoming Self-Loathing and Insecurity

I can certainly empathize with how deeply rooted issues of self-loathing and insecurity can be! At the core, those grandiose displays of superiority and arrogance mask profound feelings of inadequacy that have been aching since childhood.

When a child's sense of self-worth becomes inextricably tethered to achievements or living up to lofty expectations, it instills this brutal belief that you're only lovable or valid when you're exceptional. That inner voice of "I'm not enough" gets amplified with every perceived failure or imperfection, setting the stage for ruthless self-judgment.

And in today's societal culture that glorifies wealth, status, and conventional success metrics above all else? Those ingrained insecurities only get compounded by the relentless pressures to obtain some sort of flawless ideal. Perpetually feeling like you have to measure up breeds this endless cycle of burnout striving for the next accomplishment high, followed by that crushing self-loathing comedown when you inevitably fall short of perfection.

I know I fell into that toxic comparison trap hardcore. Always sizing myself up against others' career milestones or relationship statuses on social media. No matter how much I achieved, it never felt sufficient because there was always someone outperforming me, leaving me swimming in feelings of inadequacy and jealousy.

The brutal irony is that all those narcissistic overcompensation behaviors like arrogance, boastfulness, and excessive people-pleasing ultimately become self-sabotaging coping mechanisms that corrode our ability to form genuine connections and cultivate lasting self-esteem from within. We end up alienating others with our neediness for validation, our refusal to ever be vulnerable enough to have our true selves seen and accepted.

But here's the thing—those deep-rooted insecurities and that inexhaustible self-critical voice don't have to hold dominion over our lives indefinitely. Unpacking the origins of those wounds through self-reflection, potentially working with a therapist, and incorporating self-compassion practices—those are the paths forward.

The more we're able to build authentic self-worth independent of society's yardsticks for success, the more liberated we become. Imagine being comfortable in your own skin, not constantly craving external validation or living in fear that your flaws will be exposed. Or having the resilience to take constructive criticism or setbacks not as indictments on your self-worth, but as growth opportunities. That freedom from the shackles of self-loathing and chronic insecurity? That's what meaningful joy and fulfillment are made of.

Identifying Sources of Self-Loathing and Insecurity

It's so important to start unpacking where those feelings of self-loathing and insecurity are truly stemming from. Those harsh negative voices we hear echoing in our minds didn't just spontaneously appear—they took root from very real experiences and circumstances that planted those seeds of self-doubt.

For many of us, those damaging self-beliefs can be traced back to childhood trauma, whether it was being relentlessly criticized, emotionally neglected, or suffering abuse of any kind. Those experiences instill a profoundly painful feeling from such a young age of being fundamentally unworthy or unlovable. No wonder the adult inclination becomes overcompensating with narcissistic entitlement and demands for excessive validation— it's a desperate attempt to finally get the acceptance and admiration that was so cruelly withheld.

But even without that level of early trauma, simply being the target of bullying or constantly compared to siblings or peers can leave lasting self-esteem scars. Those memories of never feeling adequate or being repeatedly mocked get internalized as that persistent inner critic voice telling you "you're not good enough" or "you always fail." It becomes this brutal cycle where any mistake or shortcoming feels like irrefutable proof of your lack of self-worth.

For those with narcissistic tendencies in particular, that insecurity fuels this compulsive need to prove ourselves superior to others at all costs. We start catastrophizing any misstep as proof of our inadequacy, overgeneralizing that one failure into a self-fulfilling prophecy of inevitable defeat. Or we arrogantly dismiss any compliments or successes because deep down, we've convinced ourselves they're hollow and don't truly "count."

The roots of self-loathing can vary but often include:

- Childhood trauma (abuse, neglect, excessive criticism)
- Bullying/peer rejection
- Conditioning that love/worth is contingent on achievement
- Societal/cultural pressures for perfection

Unpacking those origins through self-reflection, journaling on recurring thought patterns, and getting outside perspective from a counselor when needed—that's where the real work begins. Because until we can interrupt that cycle of negative self-talk fueled by those toxic core beliefs about ourselves, that familiar self-loathing will keep weighing us down.

Those are excellent journal prompts for doing that courageous inner work to uproot the origins of self-loathing and insecurity:

Think back to your childhood. Were there specific events or relationships that made you feel unworthy or inadequate? How do these memories affect your self-view today?

Write down some of the negative things you often say to yourself. How do these thoughts make you feel? What evidence do you have that contradicts these thoughts?

Reflect on moments when you present a facade of confidence. What are you trying to protect or hide? How does this facade affect your relationships?

Reflect on your need for external validation. How often do you seek approval from others, and why? How does this behavior impact your self-esteem and relationships?

Common Insecurities in Narcissistic Individuals

Fear of Failure

- Manifestation: Narcissistic individuals might avoid tasks where success isn't guaranteed or might excessively highlight their achievements to overshadow potential failures.
- Perception by Others: This can come off as arrogance or overconfidence, leading others to view them as boastful or unwilling to engage in teamwork.
- Effects: This behavior can isolate them from peers, create resentment, and ultimately prevent genuine personal and professional growth.

Need for Approval

- Manifestation: Constantly seeking praise and validation, they might manipulate situations to receive compliments or may react negatively to criticism.

- Perception by Others: Others may perceive them as needy or insecure, which can be off-putting and lead to strained relationships.
- Effects: This need can create a cycle of dependency on others' opinions, hindering true self-esteem development.

Imposter Syndrome

- Manifestation: Despite external successes, they might feel like frauds and fear being exposed as incompetent.
- Perception by Others: This might not be overtly visible but can lead to overcompensation, making them appear boastful or disingenuous.
- Effects: This can result in chronic anxiety and prevent them from taking on new challenges or responsibilities.

Inadequacy in Relationships

- Manifestation: They may constantly compare themselves to others, leading to jealousy and possessiveness in relationships.
- Perception by Others: Partners and friends may see them as overly controlling or insecure, which can damage trust and intimacy.
- Effects: This behavior can lead to toxic relationships and emotional distress for both parties.

Perfectionism

- Manifestation: They might set unrealistically high standards for themselves and others, becoming critical and unforgiving of mistakes.
- Perception by Others: This can make them seem harsh or unapproachable, creating tension in personal and professional relationships.
- Effects: Perfectionism can lead to burnout, dissatisfaction, and a perpetual sense of failure.

Strategies for Building Self-Esteem

Building authentic self-esteem from the inside out is a pivotal part of breaking those toxic cycles of self-loathing and narcissistic overcompensation. For so long, many of us have been chasing external validation and achievements as flimsy replacements for true self-worth. But it's an endless, dissatisfying treadmill that will never provide the unshakable security and sense of enoughness we crave.

I get how confronting just how fragile your self-esteem really is can feel like a gut-punch at first. There's a reason those harsh negative tapes play on repeat in our minds—acknowledging their destructive mantras opens up vulnerabilities we've spent years masterfully avoiding.

Do the following feel all too familiar?

- You find yourself needing constant validation
- You often feel inadequate or fear criticism

If so, those are clear indicators that your sense of self-worth is largely derived from external sources rather than an internal foundation of self-acceptance. And it makes total sense why we developed those inclinations, based on our unique experiences and negative conditioning.

But perpetually leaning on others' approval, no matter how much we may crave it, is an unsustainable way to cultivate lasting esteem and emotional resilience. At some point, we have to start parenting ourselves with the compassion and unconditional positive regard we've been so desperately seeking from the outside world.

The great news is, this journey of building solid, healthy self-esteem is absolutely an inside job we all have the power to undertake, one step at a time. It involves:

- Noticing and interrupting those negative self-talk loops when they arise
- Gradually replacing harsh self-criticism with self-compassion
- Celebrating small wins and focusing on personal growth over recognition
- Learning to accept and integrate positive feedback graciously
- Separating your sense of worth from any single achievement or failure

It's a conscious practice of deprogramming those old tapes that tell us we're unworthy or inadequate. Of forging a new, more loving, and nurturing relationship with ourselves based on reality rather than distorted self-perceptions.

I spent years dismissing compliments as wishful thinking or insisting "it's not that simple" when loved ones pointed out my rigid manner. The reality? Relinquishing a defensive attitude and owning my role in projecting impossibly high expectations was pivotal.

Rather than shut down, I embraced the vulnerability of self-reflection. I got honest about how coping with childhood voices of authority and wisdom through an adult life script of criticism and control was not helpful. Unpacking why I lashed out when loved ones challenged my know-it-all tendencies was crucial.

For so long, I was the guy always responding, "Ugh, yes, thanks for the helpful critique, beloved," while inwardly feeling exposed by those words. Fears about "failing" fueled recklessness, validating flaws, and making assumptions. But the more I invited warmth and looked at those willing to question firm judgments with love, I saw why reenacting judgmental grandeur through endless skepticism is dehumanizing. Growth needs room to breathe.

I've had to actively disinvite that internal cynic when it comes to examining toxic coping mechanisms. Whether it's my harsh inner voice that acts out, discredits others' joy, or resists facing its own reflection, cultivating closure frequently is an inside job. Are you willing to lovingly own why making space for transformation can be its own reward, beloved? It's hard work facing closure but it feels life-giving.

The solution? Stay vigilant about recognizing that wisdom in your voice. My self-discovery is an endless course and journey navigating self-love. The more I embrace vulnerability, the more clearly I can value reality over resistance. I'm opening up to limitless growth when I let go and accept the process and appreciate the evolution of exploring growth through the practice of being 'overheard.'

Is it challenging work that requires diligence? For sure. Our default habits of self-flagellation can be stubborn riptides working against us. But committing to esteeming ourselves, flaws and all, is truly the greatest gift. One that opens up profound emotional freedom and a future of deeper, more fulfilling connections with ourselves and others.

Let's explore some practical strategies for building self-esteem that can help. You don't have to take them all—just select the ones that resonate with you and feel manageable.

Positive Affirmations and Self-Compassion: Positive affirmations can help rewire your brain to focus on your strengths and potential. Repeating affirmations like "I am worthy of love and respect" or "I am capable of achieving my goals" can gradually shift your self-perception. Alongside affirmations, practice self-compassion. Treat yourself with the same kindness and understanding you would offer a friend who is struggling.

Setting and Achieving Personal Goals: Setting and achieving personal goals, no matter how small, can boost your sense of competence and self-worth. Start with manageable goals that align with your interests and values. Achieving these goals provides a sense of accomplishment and motivation to continue growing.

Building Competence and Skills: Investing time in developing new skills or enhancing existing ones can significantly boost your confidence. Whether it's learning a new language, picking up a hobby, or improving your professional skills, building competence in various areas of your life can help you feel more capable and secure.

Seeking Positive Feedback and Validation: Surround yourself with supportive people who provide positive feedback and validation. Constructive criticism is valuable, but it's also important to hear about your strengths and successes. Seek out friends, family, or mentors who uplift and encourage you.

Addressing Underlying Issues: To truly overcome self-loathing and insecurity, it's essential to address the underlying issues that contribute to these feelings. This often involves delving into your past and understanding how it shapes your present self-perception.

Exploring Past Traumas and Their Impact: Past traumas can have a lasting impact on self-esteem. Therapy can provide a safe space to explore these traumas, understand their effects, and work through unresolved emotions. Healing from past traumas can release the hold they have on your self-perception and help you move forward with greater confidence.

Developing a Self-Care Routine: Self-care is crucial for maintaining mental and emotional well-being. Develop a routine that includes activities that nourish your body, mind, and soul. This might include regular exercise, healthy eating, adequate sleep, and time for relaxation and hobbies. Taking care of yourself sends a powerful message that you are worthy of care and attention.

Mindfulness and Self-Awareness Practices: Mindfulness practices can help you become more aware of your thoughts and feelings without judgment. Techniques such as meditation, deep breathing, and mindful journaling can help you stay present and reduce the impact of negative thought patterns. By increasing self-awareness, you can better understand and manage your emotions.

DEFINITION OF TRAUMA

Trauma, in its simplest form, refers to any experience that completely overwhelms your ability to cope at that moment. It goes beyond just a bad day or tough life phase—trauma is that profound sense of fear, powerlessness, or horror in the face of something utterly unraveling your sense of safety and stability.

For some, it's a singular traumatic event, often referred to as "big T" trauma, such as surviving a violent attack, natural disaster, or horrific accident. These are experiences so shocking and distressing that your psyche doesn't have the inner resources to process them fully in real-time. The memories and visceral emotions get stuck on a continuous loop, replaying in your mind through nightmares, flashbacks, and unshakable anxiety.

On the other hand, "small t" trauma refers to less intense but still significant experiences that can accumulate over time. These might include ongoing emotional neglect, constant criticism, or repeated instances of feeling unsafe. While these smaller events may not seem as immediately devastating as a single catastrophic incident, their cumulative effect can be equally profound, leading to chronic stress, anxiety, and long-term emotional difficulties.

On an emotional level, that residual trauma shapes people's self-worth, ability to trust, and capacity for intimacy in relationships. Old fears of being unlovable or fundamentally unsafe in the world get deeply encoded in our psyches and relational patterns when trauma isn't reckoned with head-on through professional support or personal inner work.

Trauma's Influence on Personality and Behavior

Trauma can have a profoundly shaping influence on personality development and coping behaviors, including narcissistic traits. When the psyche has been shattered by experiences of deep fear, vulnerability, and helplessness, it makes sense that overcompensating strategies get unconsciously adopted to regain a sense of control and self-preservation.

For someone carrying unprocessed childhood trauma from abuse, neglect, or violence, that primal feeling of being overwhelmed and lacking safety gets encoded at the core of their identity. So narcissistic defenses like grandiosity, entitlement, and lack of empathy emerge as armoring against ever feeling that level of fragility again. The superiority complex acts as an ego shield, while the inability to attune to others' emotional worlds stems from having to fundamentally disconnect from one's own inner emotional truth as a means of psychic survival.

I know for me, developing those narcissistic coping mechanisms allowed me to avoid confronting the anguish and attachment wounds left by my mom's persistent emotional unavailability and criticism growing up. If I could just achieve enough, earn enough praise from others, I could sidestep that universal fear of being fundamentally unlovable that our traumas reinforce. Pretending I didn't have needs allowed me to detach from vulnerability.

The difficult truth is that no amount of posturing, controlling behavior, or social praise-seeking can ever resolve the root injuries we're trying so desperately to numb out or compensate for. Those traumas remain trapped in the unconscious psyche, playing on an inescapable loop until we develop the self-awareness and courage to finally face them head-on.

Only by going inward, processing those fears and emotions we disconnected from so long ago, can we slowly dismantle the narcissistic defenses and develop more secure self-worth and empathic capacity. It's the hardest inner work, but getting free from the protective yet toxic overcompensations is where the possibility for healing resides.

Types of Trauma

Let me share with you my personal journey through understanding the different types of trauma and how they can shape narcissistic traits. This awareness comes from years of self-reflection and analysis. It's a complex topic, but one that's crucial for anyone looking to understand and overcome these behaviors.

Let's start with acute trauma. This is the kind of trauma that comes from a single, overwhelming event. I remember when I was in a car accident a few years back. It was sudden, intense, and left me feeling vulnerable and out of control. In the aftermath, I found myself becoming hyper-focused on maintaining an image of strength and invulnerability. I didn't want anyone to see how shaken I really was.

I started exaggerating my accomplishments, talking constantly about how well I was handling everything. Looking back, I can see how I was using these behaviors to counter those feelings of helplessness and vulnerability. It was my way of saying, "See? I'm fine. I'm strong. Nothing can touch me." But in reality, I was masking my true feelings and pushing people away.

Then there's chronic trauma, which is more prolonged and repeated. For me, this came in the form of growing up with a parent who was emotionally unpredictable. I never knew what kind of mood they'd be in, whether I'd be praised or criticized. Over time, I developed this deep-seated need for control and admiration as a way to cope with the constant stress and fear.

I became hyper-vigilant about how others perceived me. I'd go to great lengths to present a perfect image to the world, always striving to be the best, the most successful, the most put-together. It was exhausting, but it felt safer than allowing myself to be vulnerable or to admit that I was struggling.

Complex trauma is perhaps the trickiest to understand. It involves exposure to multiple traumatic events, often of an interpersonal nature. In my case, it was a combination of childhood neglect and bullying at school. This double whammy left me with a deeply distorted self-perception and a tendency to use manipulation as a means of maintaining control.

I developed this grandiose self-image as a defense mechanism. If I could convince myself (and others) that I was exceptional, then maybe I could escape the feelings of worthlessness and shame that plagued me. I became skilled at reading people and situations, always looking for ways to come out on top, to be the center of attention.

These coping mechanisms—the need for admiration, the lack of empathy, the manipulative behaviors—they all served a purpose at one time. They were my mind's way of protecting me from further hurt. But as I've come to realize, they also kept me from forming genuine connections and living authentically.

Recognizing the link between my past traumas and my narcissistic traits was a game-changer for me. It allowed me to see these behaviors not as an unchangeable part of who I am, but as learned responses that I could unlearn.

This awareness opened the door to real healing. It hasn't been easy. There are still days when I catch myself slipping into old patterns, especially when I'm feeling stressed or vulnerable. But now I have the tools to recognize what's happening and redirect myself.

I know you are on a similar journey and I want you to know that change is possible. Understanding the roots of your behaviors doesn't excuse them, but it does provide a roadmap for growth. It's okay to acknowledge that you've been hurt, that you've developed these traits as a way to protect yourself. The key is to recognize when these coping mechanisms are no longer serving you and to be willing to do the hard work of changing them.

How Past Trauma Can Contribute to Narcissistic Behaviors

When you experience deep wounds as a kid, especially from the people who were supposed to nurture and protect you, it's only natural that your mind starts building defense mechanisms to shield you from further emotional pain. Narcissistic behaviors often emerge this way - as intuitive self-preservation tactics.

For example, imagine growing up in an abusive household where your sense of self-worth was constantly being shattered by parents or caregivers. Is it any wonder you might latch onto an overinflated, grandiose self-image to try to counteract those crippling feelings of worthlessness? Or that you'd become incapable of true empathy as a means of disconnecting from your own unrelenting emotional anguish?

These narcissistic adaptations - entitlement, lack of empathy, desperate needs for validation - don't just disappear once the childhood trauma ends. Those hardwired coping strategies persist into adulthood, shaping how we move through relationships and view ourselves at the core.

It means those toxic patterns don't define your identity - they simply represent intuitive responses to past hurt. Once you can accept narcissism as an understandable survival technique, you open the door to changing those entrenched cycles. So, the first step is exploring exactly how your specific childhood experiences of neglect, abuse, or emotional deprivation contributed to narcissistic wiring.

Neglect. Neglect occurs when a child's basic needs for physical, emotional, and psychological care are not met. This can include insufficient food, lack of supervision, or emotional disengagement from caregivers. When children are neglected, they may develop narcissistic traits as a way to cope with feelings of worthlessness and abandonment.

For example, imagine a child named Alex who often comes home to an empty house because his parents are frequently absent due to work commitments or personal issues. Alex receives little to no attention or affection, and as a result, he learns to rely solely on himself, viewing his own needs as the most important. Growing up feeling invisible and unimportant, Alex might compensate by developing an inflated sense of self-importance, constantly seeking admiration and validation from others to fill the void left by his neglectful parents.

Abuse. Abuse can be physical, emotional, or sexual, and it profoundly affects a child's development. Children who experience abuse may develop narcissistic traits as a defense mechanism to shield themselves from intense feelings of shame, fear, and helplessness.

Consider a child named Mia who is regularly subjected to harsh criticism and physical punishment by her parents. They belittle her accomplishments and use derogatory language. To survive this toxic environment, Mia creates a persona of invulnerability. As a result, she may grow up suppressing her true feelings and adopting a facade of superiority to hide her deep-seated insecurities. Mia might become highly critical of others, unable to empathize, and constantly seek power and control in relationships to avoid feeling vulnerable again.

Lack of Emotional Support. A lack of emotional support involves caregivers being emotionally unavailable or unresponsive to a child's needs. This might manifest as indifference, minimal affection, or a failure to provide encouragement and validation. Without emotional support, children may develop narcissistic traits as a way to gain the attention and approval they crave.

Imagine a child named Jake whose parents are physically present but emotionally distant. They rarely praise his efforts or show interest in his feelings and experiences, leaving Jake feeling unseen and unheard. Struggling to get their attention, Jake might grow up feeling unworthy of love, constantly striving to prove his worth. He may become overly focused on achievements and external validation, developing narcissistic behaviors such as bragging and seeking admiration to compensate for his emotional deprivation.

Narcissistic Coping Mechanisms

Understanding the most common coping mechanisms used by folks with narcissistic tendencies can shed light on why we act the way we do and help guide the healing process.

Hyper-Focus on Image and Achievements

Explanation: To counter feelings of vulnerability and helplessness resulting from the acute trauma, individuals may develop a hyper-focus on their image and achievements. This helps them regain a sense of control and self-worth.

Example: After surviving a violent attack, an individual might become obsessively focused on their physical appearance and career accomplishments, seeking constant validation and admiration from others to reinforce their sense of strength and resilience.

Seeking Constant Validation

Explanation: Acute trauma can shatter an individual's self-esteem, leading them to seek external validation as a way to rebuild their self-worth.

Example: Following a traumatic event like a car accident, someone might become excessively reliant on praise and approval from others, constantly seeking reassurance of their value and significance.

Exaggerated Self-Importance

Explanation: To manage the constant fear and anxiety associated with chronic trauma, individuals might develop an exaggerated sense of self-importance. This grandiosity serves as a defense mechanism to cope with their ongoing emotional pain.

Example: Growing up in a home with domestic violence, a child might adopt an inflated self-view, believing they are superior to others. This helps them feel powerful and in control, countering the helplessness they experience in their environment.

Lack of Empathy

Explanation: Chronic trauma can lead to emotional numbing as a coping strategy. This lack of empathy allows individuals to disconnect from their own pain and avoid being overwhelmed by the suffering of others.

Example: Someone who has experienced repeated emotional abuse may become desensitized to others' emotions, focusing solely on their own needs and desires to protect themselves from further hurt.

Control and Manipulation

Explanation: To survive in an unpredictable and threatening environment, individuals with chronic trauma might resort to controlling and manipulative behaviors. This ensures they can manage their surroundings and reduce their sense of vulnerability.
Example: A person who endured prolonged bullying at school might develop manipulative tactics to control social situations and ensure they are always in a position of power, preventing others from causing them harm.

Grandiose Self-Image

Explanation: To cope with profound emotional pain and confusion caused by repeated trauma, individuals might create a grandiose self-image. This inflated sense of self serves as a shield against their damaged sense of self-worth.
Example: A child who faced multiple forms of abuse might grow up believing they are exceptionally talented and deserving of special treatment. This grandiosity helps them mask their deep-seated insecurities and maintain a sense of control.

Manipulative Behaviors

Explanation: Complex trauma can severely disrupt an individual's sense of identity and trust in others. As a result, they may use manipulation to navigate their relationships and maintain a sense of security.
Example: An adult who experienced childhood neglect might use charm and deceit to manipulate others into meeting their needs. This behavior stems from a lack of trust and a need to control their environment to avoid feeling abandoned again.

Emotional Numbing and Detachment

Explanation: To protect themselves from overwhelming emotional pain, individuals with complex trauma might detach emotionally. This detachment can manifest as a lack of empathy and an inability to connect deeply with others.
Example: A person who grew up in a chaotic and abusive household may find it difficult to form genuine emotional connections, often appearing cold and indifferent to others' feelings.

The Healing Process

Healing from trauma isn't a straightforward path—it's more like a winding road with its fair share of bumps and detours. But understanding the journey can make it a bit easier to navigate. Let's break it down into stages and talk about how having a solid support system can make all the difference.

1. Initial Recognition and Acceptance

Let's talk about the first big step in healing from trauma—recognizing and accepting what happened to you. This part? It's often the toughest. It's like finally opening a door you've kept locked for years, knowing there's a whirlwind of painful memories and emotions waiting on the other side.

For those of us who've developed narcissistic traits, this stage can feel particularly threatening. We've often built up these elaborate defenses to protect our fragile self-esteem. The idea of confronting our trauma? It can feel like we're taking a sledgehammer to the carefully constructed image we've created of ourselves.

But here's the thing—accepting your trauma doesn't mean you're okay with what happened. It just means you're acknowledging its impact on your life and you're ready to start dealing with it. It's like saying, "Yes, this happened to me, and yes, it's affected me in ways I need to address."

During this stage, don't be surprised if you start experiencing flashbacks, nightmares, or intense emotions that seem to come out of nowhere. These reactions can be really jarring, especially if they clash with the strong, invulnerable image you've been projecting. Remember, though, these are normal responses to trauma. They don't make you weak—they make you human.

This is where professional help can be a game-changer. A good therapist can provide a safe space for you to explore these feelings and start the healing process. They can help you navigate the discomfort of facing these truths and offer strategies to cope with the emotional rollercoaster you might find yourself on.

2. Processing and Understanding Trauma

Once you've taken that first big step of recognizing and accepting your trauma, it's time to roll up your sleeves and really dig into understanding it. This stage is all about exploring the details of what happened to you and how it's shaped your thoughts, emotions, and behaviors.

I won't sugarcoat it—It's like cleaning out an infected wound. It hurts, but it's necessary for healing. It's where we start to break down that facade of superiority and really look at the insecurities driving our behaviors.

Processing your trauma might involve talking it through with a therapist or writing about it in a journal. The goal is to make sense of what happened and how it's affected you. This can be particularly challenging if you're used to maintaining a certain image of yourself. It requires vulnerability and a willingness to look beyond the inflated self-image you might have created.

As you work through this stage, you might start to see connections between your trauma and your current behaviors. Maybe you'll realize that certain things trigger your anxiety, or that you've developed coping mechanisms that aren't really serving you anymore—like constantly seeking validation or getting defensive at the slightest criticism.

This stage is all about gaining insight. It's about understanding where your narcissistic tendencies come from. And while it can be uncomfortable, it's also incredibly empowering. It gives you the knowledge you need to start making positive changes in your life.

3. Rebuilding and Moving Forward

Now we come to the final stage of healing—rebuilding your life and moving forward. This is where you take everything you've learned about yourself and your trauma and use it to create a new sense of normalcy. It is about finding ways to integrate our trauma into our life story without letting it define us. It's about developing a healthier, more balanced self-image.

Rebuilding might involve setting new goals for yourself, working on fostering healthier relationships, or engaging in activities that bring you genuine joy and fulfillment. The key here is shifting your focus from external validation to internal growth and satisfaction.

This stage also involves developing new coping strategies. You might explore mindfulness practices, pick up new hobbies, or seek out experiences that challenge and enrich you. The goal is to build a toolkit of healthy ways to deal with stress and emotions.

One of the biggest parts of this stage is learning to trust again—both yourself and others. It's about rebuilding your self-esteem and confidence that might have been shattered by your trauma. This stage involves moving beyond the need for constant admiration and developing a genuine sense of self-worth. It's about recognizing that you haven't just endured trauma—you've grown stronger from it. This newfound strength and self-awareness can enable you to form more authentic and fulfilling relationships.

Healing isn't a linear process. You might find yourself cycling through these stages or revisiting certain aspects. That's okay. What matters is that you're on the path. Every step forward, no matter how small, is a victory. You're reclaiming your life, your relationships, and your authentic self.

How to Approach Therapy

There's still a lot of stigma around seeking therapy. Many people see it as a sign of weakness or think they should be able to handle their problems on their own. But here's the truth: asking for help is a sign of strength. It shows that you're committed to your personal growth and willing to do the hard work of healing.

Seeking therapy is a big step, and it takes a lot of courage. It's like opening a door to a room you've kept locked for a long time—it can feel scary, but it's also the first step toward healing and growth.

But, we tend to have a tendency...let's talk about one of the biggest hurdles you might face in therapy: the tendency to lie or gaslight the therapist. It's a common challenge for people with narcissistic traits, often stemming from fear. You might be afraid of being vulnerable, of having your carefully constructed self-image challenged, or of facing painful truths about yourself.

Here's the thing: honesty in therapy is crucial. It's like trying to navigate a ship—if you don't give the captain (your therapist) accurate information, you're not going to reach your destination. So how do you stay honest and open in therapy?

1. First, set clear intentions before each session. Remind yourself why you're there and what you hope to achieve. Maybe even write down specific topics or feelings you want to address. This can help keep you focused and committed to honesty.

2. Consider keeping a therapy journal. After each session, jot down what you discussed and reflect on how honest you were. This can help you stay accountable to yourself and track your progress over time.

3. Practice vulnerability. I know it's scary, but try to gradually open up about your feelings and experiences. Start small with less threatening topics and work your way up to the bigger stuff. Remember, your therapist is there to support you, not judge you.

4. Don't be afraid to ask your therapist for feedback on your progress and honesty. They can help you recognize when you might be deflecting or withholding information and work with you to address these tendencies.

5. Mindfulness exercises can be really helpful too. They can make you more aware of your thoughts and feelings, which can help you recognize when you're tempted to lie or deflect in therapy.

Therapy can bring about amazing changes in your life. It can help you develop healthier communication skills, which can transform your relationships. It can also increase your capacity for empathy, and by addressing the root causes of your issues and learning coping strategies, you can alleviate many of the symptoms that interfere with your daily life.

Therapeutic Approaches

Choosing the right therapist is crucial. Look for someone who specializes in treating narcissistic traits and trauma. You want someone who has experience in these areas and understands what you're going through. Trust your gut feeling too—if you feel comfortable with a therapist and feel like they really hear you, that's a good sign.

I'm going to share what works for me, but remember, what works for one person might not work for another. It's about finding the right combination of approaches that resonate with you.

First up, Cognitive Behavioral Therapy (CBT). Think of CBT as a way to rewire your brain. It's all about understanding how your thoughts, feelings, and behaviors are interconnected, and then learning how to change the patterns that aren't serving you well.

It helps you tackle those negative beliefs and fears that often come hand-in-hand with traumatic experiences. You know those grandiose self-perceptions and unrealistic expectations you might have developed? CBT gives you the tools to build a more balanced, realistic view of yourself and the world around you. It's about finding a middle ground between the extremes of grandiosity and self-loathing.

Next, Eye Movement Desensitization and Reprocessing (EMDR). I know, it's a mouthful, but bear with me because this therapy can be incredibly powerful. EMDR is like a reset button for your traumatic memories. It involves recalling these memories while following guided eye movements. It might sound strange, but this process can help you reprocess the memories underlying your need for control and admiration. As these memories lose their sting, you might find your defensive behaviors becoming less intense and less necessary.

There are various other techniques that can support your healing journey. Mindfulness practices, for instance, can help you stay grounded in the present moment, reducing anxiety about the past or future. Relaxation exercises can give you tools to manage stress and overwhelming emotions.

Don't underestimate the power of expressive therapies either. Art therapy, music therapy—these aren't just for kids. They can be incredibly powerful ways to process emotions that are hard to put into words. Sometimes, picking up a paintbrush or sitting down at a piano can unlock feelings and memories in a way that talking just can't.

Now, let's dive into some practical strategies to support this journey.

Self-care is absolutely crucial. It's not selfish—it's necessary. Think of it as maintenance for your mind, body, and soul. This includes physical self-care like regular exercise, a balanced diet, and getting enough sleep. But it's also about emotional self-care—doing things that bring you joy and help you relax. And don't forget mental self-care—keeping your mind engaged and challenged.

Mindfulness and meditation are powerful tools in this journey. They help you stay present and connected to your thoughts and feelings without judgment. Start small—maybe with a few minutes of mindful breathing each day. As you get more comfortable, you can try practices like body scans or loving-kindness meditation.

Building resilience is another key component. Life is going to throw challenges your way—that's inevitable. Resilience is about how you bounce back from these challenges. It's about maintaining a positive outlook, even when things get tough. Practice gratitude, reframe negative thoughts, and try to view setbacks as opportunities for growth.

To conclude, don't be afraid to try different techniques or to ask for help in finding the right therapeutic approach. And remember, this is a journey of continuous personal development where you're uncovering the best version of yourself—one that's capable of genuine connections, empathy, and self-love.

HEALING YOUR INNER CHILD

Inner child work is one of the most powerful ways to heal from childhood trauma and transform narcissistic traits. This concept might sound a bit new-age or touchy-feely at first, but it's rooted in serious psychological research and can be incredibly transformative.

The idea of the "inner child" has deep roots in psychology, going all the way back to Carl Jung in the early 20th century. Jung talked about the "child archetype" as this innocent, spontaneous part of our psyche. But it was John Bradshaw who really brought this concept into the mainstream in the 1980s with his book "Homecoming: Reclaiming and Healing Your Inner Child."

So what exactly is this inner child? Think of it as the part of you that holds your earliest memories, emotions, and experiences. It's not just about the happy, carefree moments of childhood—though those are certainly part of it. It's also about the hurts, the fears, the anger, and the sadness that you might have experienced as a kid.

For those of us who've developed narcissistic traits, this inner child often carries some pretty deep wounds. As a consequence, some of us learned to disconnect from our emotions entirely as a survival mechanism. This emotional numbing might have helped you cope as a child, but in adulthood, it can show up as a lack of empathy—a hallmark of narcissistic behavior.

The beautiful thing about inner child work is that it gives us a chance to heal these old wounds. It's about reconnecting with that younger version of yourself, acknowledging the pain and the unmet needs, and giving yourself the love, support, and nurturing that you might have missed out on.

This process can be incredibly powerful as we become more self-aware, more in tune with our triggers and responses-leading to better emotional regulation and a deeper understanding of ourselves.

As we heal our inner child, we often find that we're naturally developing more empathy and emotional awareness. We're less likely to dismiss or ignore others' emotions because we're more in touch with our own. We start to build a genuine sense of self-worth that doesn't rely on constant external validation.

One of the most beautiful outcomes of this work is that we can start to shed those defensive layers of grandiosity and control. We can embrace our true selves, leading to more authentic and fulfilling relationships with others.

In fact, one of the most profound benefits of inner child work is the opportunity to embrace your true self: The part of you that exists beyond the need for external validation and grandiosity. It is the version of you that is capable of genuine connections, empathy, and self-worth that is not contingent on the opinions of others. Embracing your true self involves acknowledging and accepting all parts of you, including your vulnerabilities, imperfections, and past traumas.

This process is about grounding yourself in reality and authenticity. When you embrace your true self, you are no longer reliant on a facade to interact with the world. This authenticity allows for more meaningful and fulfilling relationships, as others are able to connect with the real you, not just the image you project.

Now, I won't sugarcoat it—this process isn't always easy. It requires patience, compassion, and a willingness to face some uncomfortable truths. You might have to confront memories or feelings that you've been avoiding for years. But I promise you, it's worth it.

If you're interested in diving deeper into this work, I'd highly recommend checking out "Your Inner Child Healing Journey" by Samantha Jones. It's a fantastic workbook that's helped many people on their path to recovery. Additionally, if you want to explore Carl Jung's archetypes and work on meeting your true self, "The Shadow Work Journal and Workbook: How to Meet Your True Self" by Samantha Jones is an excellent resource.

From Wounds to Wisdom

In inner child work, we uncover the experiences that shaped us and then rebuild on healthier, more solid ground. It's quite a journey, and I've broken it down into several key stages. Let's walk through them together.

Identifying and Acknowledging Childhood Wounds

I'll be honest with you—this part isn't easy. Looking inward and addressing past wounds can be painful, but it's also where the real growth happens. When I first started this process, I was amazed at how much of my adult life was influenced by experiences I thought I'd long forgotten.

So, how do we do this? Well, it starts with reflection, recognizing our unmet needs, and acknowledging our feelings. These steps help us break down the walls that narcissism built, opening the door to self-awareness. Let's dive in.

Reflecting on Past Experiences

First things first—we need to create a safe space for ourselves. No judgment allowed here. Think back to your earliest memories. What moments stand out? Maybe times when you felt neglected, harshly criticized, or misunderstood?

Don't be discouraged if the first time you try this exercise you end up staring at a blank page. It can take time to access these memories and feelings, especially if you've spent years burying them. Be patient with yourself and keep trying.

I remember when I first did this exercise. It was tough but illuminating. I realized how much a seemingly small incident—my father missing my school play—had affected me. What about you? What memories surface?

Journaling Prompts

- *What are some of your earliest childhood memories? How do these memories make you feel today?*

- *Describe a specific instance in your childhood where you felt hurt or neglected. How did it affect you then and how does it affect you now?*

Recognizing Unmet Needs

Here's the thing about children—they need love, validation, security, and acceptance to develop a healthy sense of self. When these needs aren't met, it can lead to all sorts of issues down the line.

Ask yourself: What emotional needs went unfulfilled in your childhood? How do you see these playing out in your adult life? For me, I realized I was constantly seeking approval from others because I didn't get enough validation as a kid. Sound familiar?

Journaling Prompts

- *What emotional needs were not met in your childhood? How do you see these unmet needs manifesting in your current behaviors and relationships?*

- *Reflect on a time when you felt particularly unloved or unsupported. How did you cope with those feelings then, and how do you cope with similar feelings now?*

Acknowledging Feelings

Now comes the part that many of us struggle with. We've gotten really good at suppressing our emotions, haven't we? But here's the truth: healing requires us to reconnect with these feelings, no matter how uncomfortable they might be.

Start by naming the emotions that come up when you think about your childhood wounds. Anger? Sadness? Fear? Shame? Whatever they are, let yourself feel them. It's okay, I promise. These feelings are a natural response to your experiences.

One exercise that really helped me was writing a letter to my younger self. It allowed me to express emotions I couldn't articulate back then and offer the support I needed. Why not give it a try? Write to your younger self, offering the love and validation you needed at that time.

I remember sitting down to do it, pen in hand, feeling kind of silly at first. But, once I started writing, it was like a dam broke.

I started with "Hey little buddy," because that's what my grandpa used to call me. And suddenly, I was face to face with this scared, confused kid who just wanted to be loved and accepted. I wrote about feeling lonely, even in a room full of people. About being afraid to show weakness, always putting on this tough guy act. I told that little guy it was okay to feel scared, okay to be sad or angry. That he didn't have to be perfect all the time. I found myself writing things like, "You're stronger than you know, kid. All that stuff you're going through? It's not your fault. You're doing the best you can with what you've got."

It was hard, you know? Admitting to myself that yeah, I had it rough sometimes. That maybe I didn't get all the love and support I needed. But it was also... freeing. Like I was finally giving myself permission to be human.

I ended up telling my younger self that better days were coming. That he'd grow up to be someone who could love and be loved, who could make a difference in the world. When I finished, I was a mess. Tears, snot, the works. But I felt lighter somehow. Like I'd put down a weight I didn't even know I was carrying.

This exercise is not about wallowing in the past or blaming anyone. It's about understanding where you came from so you can choose where you're going. It's about giving yourself the compassion and understanding you might not have gotten back then.

Journaling Prompts

- *When you think about your childhood wounds, what emotions come up? Write about these feelings and any physical reactions you notice in your body.*

- *If you could speak to your younger self, what would you say? Write a letter offering the support, love, and validation you needed at that time.*

Reparenting Your Inner Child

Imagine for a moment that you could go back in time and be the perfect parent to your younger self. What would that look like? How would you treat that little version of you? That's essentially what reparenting is all about. It's like giving yourself a do-over, but from the inside out.

Here's the deal: We're taking on the role of that compassionate, attentive caregiver that maybe we didn't have growing up. It's about showering your inner child with all the care, support, and nurturing that you needed back then. Sounds a bit woo-woo, right? I thought so too at first, but trust me, it works.

Now, let me be clear—this isn't about pointing fingers at our parents or guardians. We're not here to play the blame game. This is about you taking the wheel of your own healing journey. It's about saying, "Hey, maybe I didn't get everything I needed as a kid, but I'm here now, and I've got my own back."

When I first started this process, it felt awkward. I mean, how do you parent yourself? But as I kept at it, something amazing happened. Those old wounds started to heal. I began to develop healthier ways of coping with stress. My self-esteem? It started to grow. And that constant inner turmoil? It began to settle into a sense of peace I'd never known before.

So, how do we do this reparenting thing? Don't worry, I've got some techniques up my sleeve that have worked wonders for me, and I bet they can help you too.

Daily Check-Ins: The Coffee Date with Yourself. Think of this as a daily coffee date with your inner child. I know it sounds a bit odd, but hear me out. Every morning, while I'm sipping my coffee, I take a moment to ask myself, "Hey, how are you feeling today? What do you need?" It's like checking in with a friend, except that friend is you. At first, I felt a bit silly doing this. But over time, it became a ritual I looked forward to. Some days, I realize I'm feeling anxious and need some extra self-care. Other days, I'm feeling great and ready to take on the world. The key is to respond to whatever comes up with kindness. No judgment allowed!

Create a Safe Space: Your Personal Retreat. Remember those blanket forts you used to build as a kid? Well, we're bringing that concept back, but with an adult twist. Find a corner in your home that can be your safe haven. For me, it's a cozy armchair in my bedroom. I've got a soft blanket, some scented candles, and a small shelf with my favorite books. This space is your retreat. When life gets overwhelming, or you need a moment to reconnect with your inner child, this is where you go. It's amazing how having a physical space dedicated to self-care can make such a difference.

Practice Self-Compassion: Be Your Own Best Friend. This one was a game-changer for me. We're often our own harshest critics, right? Well, it's time to flip the script. Whenever you catch yourself in a spiral of self-criticism, hit the pause button. Take a deep breath and ask yourself, "Would I talk to a friend this way?" Instead of beating yourself up, try speaking to yourself like you would to a child you love. "Hey, it's okay. You're doing your best. Mistakes happen, and that's how we learn." It feels weird at first, but trust me, it gets easier with practice.

Use Positive Affirmations: Your Personal Cheerleading Squad. Okay, I'll admit, I used to roll my eyes at affirmations. But then I gave them a shot, and wow—they really do make a difference. Start small. Pick one or two affirmations that resonate with you. Mine are "I am worthy of love and respect" and "I trust in my ability to handle life's challenges." Write these on sticky notes and plaster them where you'll see them often— your bathroom mirror, your fridge, your computer screen. Say them out loud when you see them. Yes, you might feel a bit silly at first, but keep at it. You're rewiring years of negative self-talk, and that takes time.

Set Boundaries: Your Inner Child's Bodyguard. Think of yourself as your inner child's protective big sibling or bodyguard. It's your job to keep them safe, and that means setting and maintaining healthy boundaries. This was tough for me at first. I was a chronic people-pleaser, always saying yes even when I wanted to say no. Start small. Practice saying no to little things that don't serve you. Remember, every time you say no to something that doesn't align with your values or needs, you're saying yes to yourself and your well-being.

So, which of these practices resonates with you the most? Why not pick one to focus on for a while? Give it some time to see how it feels and how it impacts your well-being. Once you feel comfortable with it, you can try incorporating another practice into your routine.

The Path to Self-Love

Healing your inner child is just the beginning. Think of it as laying the foundation for a house. Now it's time to build on that foundation, and the next floor is all about self-esteem.

Here's the thing about self-esteem when you've got narcissistic tendencies—it's like a house of cards. One wrong move, one criticism, and boom! It all comes tumbling down. But as you heal your inner child, you begin to realize that your worth isn't tied to what others think of you. It's like finding a well of value inside yourself that you never knew existed.

Now, building this genuine self-esteem? It's a process (for detailed strategies, refer to the techniques discussed in Chapter 2). For me, it started with small steps. I began to acknowledge my accomplishments, not for the praise they might bring, but for the effort I put in. I started to value my own opinions as much as (if not more than) others'. It felt strange at first, like wearing shoes on the wrong feet. But over time, it became more natural.

And then we come to the grand finale: self-love—a deep and unconditional acceptance of yourself. If self-esteem is about recognizing your worth, self-love is about embracing it fully, warts and all. It's about developing a secure and loving relationship with yourself that doesn't rely on external factors.

For someone with narcissistic traits, this can feel like learning a whole new language. We're so used to putting on a show, to being 'perfect,' that the idea of loving ourselves as we truly are can seem impossible. But let me tell you, it's not just possible—it's liberating. When you love yourself unconditionally, you no longer need to project a grandiose self-image or seek validation from others. This shift allows you to develop genuine empathy, form healthier relationships, and interact with the world from a place of authenticity and compassion.

When I first started practicing self-love, I felt like a fraud. But I kept at it. I started treating myself with the same kindness I'd show a good friend. Made a mistake? Instead of berating myself, I'd say, "Hey, it's okay. You're human. What can you learn from this?" Also, engaging in activities that nurture your passions and interests can reinforce your intrinsic value and happiness.

Now, here's how it all ties together to help with those narcissistic traits:

- Healing your inner child helps you understand where these behaviors come from. It's like shining a light on the root of the problem.
- Building genuine self-esteem reduces your need for constant external validation. You start to feel good about yourself without needing others to confirm it.
- Cultivating self-love allows you to be more authentic. You no longer need to project a perfect image because you accept yourself as you are.

This journey doesn't happen overnight. There were days when I felt like I was taking two steps forward and one step back. But each step, no matter how small, was progress.

"The Self-Love Workbook" by Frida Elowen is a great tool to have on this journey. It offers a guided 28-day journey to help you cultivate a deeper sense of self-love and acceptance. But also remember that you're not alone in this. Whether it's a therapist, a support group, or trusted friends, having people to lean on can make a world of difference.

BUILDING EMPAHY

Developing empathy has the power to break the cycle of narcissistic behavior. It's like taking off a pair of me-colored glasses and seeing the world through other people's eyes for the first time; it allows us to connect with others on a meaningful level, understand their feelings, and respond with compassion.

When you start to empathize, you're not so wrapped up in your own stuff anymore. You're not constantly trying to steer conversations back to you or fishing for compliments. Instead, you actually listen to people. You care about what they're going through. And let me tell you, it makes a world of difference in your relationships. You become less preoccupied with controlling situations or seeking approval. Instead of constantly trying to steer conversations back to you or fishing for compliments, you actually listen to people. You care about what they're going through. And let me tell you, this not only makes interactions more genuine but also helps build trust and respect.

There are different types of empathy, and they all play a part in how we connect with others.

First, there's cognitive empathy, also known as "perspective-taking". It's like being able to put yourself in someone else's shoes and understand their point of view. For us narcissists, this can be really helpful. We're so used to seeing things only from our perspective that just understanding where someone else is coming from can be eye-opening.

Then there's emotional empathy. This is when you actually feel what someone else is feeling. It's deeper than just understanding - you're right there with them emotionally. This one can be tough for us because we're so used to focusing on our own feelings. But man, when you start to really feel for others, it changes everything.

Finally, there's compassionate empathy. This is where you not only understand and feel for someone, but you want to help them too. It's about taking action, not just feeling bad for someone. For those of us who've been all about what we can get from others, this is a real shift. But it's amazing how good it feels to actually help someone else without expecting anything in return.

Improving Relationships: When you start really listening to people, really trying to understand where they're coming from, it changes everything. It's like you're building this bridge of trust between you and them. And for someone like me who used to struggle with trust issues, it's been eye-opening.

I remember the first time I really tried to put myself in my partner's shoes during an argument. Instead of just defending myself or trying to win, I actually tried to understand why they were upset. It was like a light bulb went off. Suddenly, we weren't fighting against each other anymore. We were working together to solve the problem.

And when you start showing people that it's okay to be vulnerable, that you're not going to judge them for their feelings, they start opening up to you in ways you never imagined. That's when relationships get really deep and meaningful.

Learning to understand other people's emotions has helped me get a handle on my own too. I used to have these intense reactions to things, you know? But now, I can step back and think, "Okay, why am I really feeling this way?" It's made a huge difference in how I handle stress and conflicts.

The best part? I don't feel so alone anymore. When you start genuinely caring about others and helping them out, you build this network of people who have your back too. And this strong network fosters resilience, making recovery from setbacks easier.

And let me tell you, there's nothing quite like the feeling you get from helping someone else, just because you can. It's not about what you get back. It's about making a difference in someone's life. That feeling? It's better than any compliment or validation I ever chased after before.

Mastering Communication: Mastering communication is about creating a two-way street where both people feel heard and understood. This is empathy in action.

Let me paint you a picture. Remember that time when you were telling your friend about your amazing weekend, and their eyes started to glaze over? Or when your partner tried to express their feelings, and you found yourself thinking about what you were going to have for dinner? Yeah, those aren't our proudest moments.

Here's the thing: effective communication is as much about listening as it is about talking. And I don't mean just waiting for your turn to speak. I'm talking about really, truly listening. It's about tuning into what the other person is saying, trying to understand their perspective, even if it's different from yours. It is about listening actively and empathetically.

For example, instead of thinking about your next brilliant point while someone else is talking, try repeating back what they've said. "So, what I'm hearing is..." This little trick does two things: it shows the other person you're really listening, and it helps you actually absorb what they're saying.

Now, let's talk about another elephant in the room: criticism. Someone points out a flaw? Time to go on the defensive! But here's a mind-blowing concept: what if we saw criticism as an opportunity for growth instead of an attack?

I remember the first time I tried this. My partner pointed out that I had a habit of interrupting them. My first instinct was to argue. But instead, I took a deep breath and said, "You're right. I didn't realize I was doing that. I'll work on it." The look of surprise on their face was priceless.

When you start communicating like this - really listening, considering other perspectives, accepting feedback - something magical happens. People start opening up to you. They trust you more. Conflicts that used to turn into World War III suddenly become manageable discussions.

For us, this shift can be nothing short of revolutionary. Suddenly, we're not constantly feeling misunderstood or at odds with everyone. We're connecting on a deeper level. We're building relationships that are actually fulfilling, not just ego-boosting.

Foundations of Effective Communication

Clear Communication: Now, I used to think I was the king of clear communication. After all, I always knew exactly what I wanted to say, right? Wrong. Turns out, there's a big difference between knowing what you want to say and actually saying it in a way others can understand.

Here's the deal: ditch the fancy words and the manipulative mind games. Just say what you mean, straight up. No beating around the bush, no hidden agendas.

I remember when I had to give feedback to a colleague. My old self would have gone in guns blazing, making it all about how their mistake affected me. But instead, I tried something new. I said, 'Hey, I noticed the report was late, which threw off our timeline. How about we set some clear deadlines to avoid this in the future?' Simple, clear, and focused on solving the problem.

The Role of Active Listening: Active listening is a crucial component of effective communication. It is like being a detective: it involves fully concentrating on the speaker, understanding their message, making eye contact, nodding along, and actually remembering what they're saying!

I'll never forget when a friend came to me with a problem. In the past, I would have immediately jumped in with my brilliant solution. But this time, I tried something different. I listened. Really listened. And then I said, 'It sounds like you're feeling really stressed about work. What can I do to help?' The look of relief on their face was priceless.

The Importance of Assertive Communication: Assertive communication is about expressing your thoughts and feelings clearly and directly while respecting others. You're balancing your own needs and feelings on one side, and respect for others on the other. It's about saying what you need to say, but in a way that doesn't steamroll over everyone else. It's the healthiest communication style because it fosters mutual respect and understanding.

This can be difficult. We usually struggle to respect others' perspectives and needs, often prioritizing our own. This can lead to behaviors that undermine healthy communication. We've got some habits to break, like interrupting people (because obviously, what we have to say is more important, right?) or dismissing their ideas (because clearly, our ideas are always the best). These habits? They shut down conversations and push people away.

So, next time you're in a situation where you need to express yourself, try the assertive approach. State your needs clearly, but also show that you're considering the other person's perspective. It might feel awkward at first, but stick with it.

Overcoming Passive Communication: Passive communication involves avoiding the expression of true thoughts and feelings, leading to resentment and unmet needs. Now you might be thinking, 'Wait a minute, I thought narcissists were all about being loud and in your face!' Well, surprise! Sometimes we slip into passive mode: we might adopt a passive communication style to avoid conflict or maintain a facade of harmony, but this often results in pent-up resentment. It's not doing us any favors.

Picture this: Your friend borrows 50 bucks from you. Weeks go by, then months. You're silently fuming, but you don't say a word. Sound familiar? I used to do this all the time. I'd tell myself, 'I'm above mentioning money,' or 'If I bring it up, they might not like me anymore.' Classic passive communication.

So why do we do this? It's often about maintaining this perfect image we've created. We want to seem unbothered, above it all. Or maybe we're afraid of conflict, worried that if we speak up, we'll shatter this illusion of harmony we've carefully constructed.

When you start communicating directly (but kindly), you're actually building stronger, more honest relationships. People know where they stand with you. There's no guesswork, no mind-reading required. It's not about winning or losing. It's about creating authentic connections

So here's your challenge: Next time you find yourself biting your tongue to keep the peace, take a deep breath and speak up instead. Be kind, be clear, and be honest about what you need or how you feel.

Addressing Aggressive Communication: Aggressive communication involves expressing thoughts and feelings in a way that violates others' rights, often leading to conflicts. We frequently exhibit aggressive communication, dominating conversations and using harsh language to assert control. Aggressive communication might feel good in the moment, like you're showing how strong you are. But in reality? It's like taking a wrecking ball to your relationships.

For example, your friend is always late. I mean always. You've planned a night out, and once again, you're standing there checking your watch every two minutes. The old you might have exploded when they finally showed up: 'You're always late! Do you even care about our plans? You're so selfish!'

Instead of going in guns blazing, we can learn to express ourselves firmly but respectfully. Let's go back to that chronically late friend. Try this on for size:

'Hey, I wanted to talk to you about something. When you're late, it really affects our plans and, honestly, it's pretty frustrating. I value our friendship and our time together. Could we agree on a time that works for both of us? That way, we can avoid this issue and enjoy our time together more.'

See the difference? We're still addressing the issue head-on, but we're doing it in a way that opens up a conversation instead of shutting it down.

Nonverbal Communication: Body language, facial expressions, and eye contact can be a real blind spots for people with narcissistic tendencies.

I remember the first time I really noticed this. I was in the middle of what I thought was a perfectly reasonable 'discussion' (okay, it was an argument) with my partner. I was making all these great points, but they just seemed to be shutting down. Then I caught a glimpse of myself in a mirror. Arms crossed, brow furrowed, looking everywhere but at them. Yikes. I looked about as approachable as a porcupine in a balloon factory.

So, let's break this down. First up: body language. When we're feeling defensive or superior (which, let's face it, can be pretty often), we tend to close ourselves off. Crossed arms, turned away, maybe even literally looking down our noses at people. Not exactly the picture of openness, right?

Instead, try this: Next time you're in a conversation, especially a tricky one, consciously open up your posture. Uncross those arms, face the person, maybe even lean in a bit. It feels vulnerable, I know. But it sends a powerful message: 'I'm here, I'm listening, and I'm engaged.'

Now, let's talk eye contact. I used to think maintaining intense eye contact was a power move. Turns out, it can make people feel like they're being interrogated. On the flip side, avoiding eye contact altogether can make you seem shifty or disinterested. The sweet spot? Regular, natural eye contact. It says, 'I see you, I hear you, and you matter.'

And don't forget about your face! We're not used to thinking about our facial expressions. But they speak volumes We might default to a neutral expression that looks... well, let's just say less than friendly. Practice softening your expression, maybe even throw in a smile now and then. It can totally change the vibe of a conversation.

Here's a challenge for you: Next time you're having a conversation, especially about something sensitive, try saying something like, 'I know this is a tough topic, but I'm here to listen and work through it together.' And while you're saying it, keep your body language open, make eye contact, and try for a gentle smile.

This isn't about manipulating people or putting on a show. It's about aligning your non-verbal cues with your words to create more genuine, empathetic connections. It's about showing people that you're not just hearing them, but you're really there with them.

Conflict Resolution: Conflict often arises from misunderstandings and a lack of perspective-taking, right? Empathy allows you to see the situation from the other person's point of view...can you see how transformative this can be? Understanding the other person's perspective can lead to more constructive discussions.

Learning to keep it cool and not get defensive, that's been tough. I used to take every bit of criticism or disagreement as a personal attack. But now, I try to remind myself that it's not about me. It's about the issue at hand. Taking that deep breath and staying calm, it's made a world of difference. Suddenly, I'm having conversations instead of arguments.

And here's the kicker - when I started seeing feedback as a chance to grow instead of an assault on my ego, it changed everything. I remember my boss gave me some pretty harsh feedback on a project. My old self would've been furious, probably would've started looking for a new job that day. But instead, I really listened to what she was saying. And you know what? She had some valid points. I used that feedback to improve, and my next project knocked it out of the park.

Finding common ground, that's been huge too. I used to be all about winning, you know? But now, I try to focus on what we both want to achieve. It's not about me vs. them anymore. It's about us working together to find a solution that works for everyone.

First up: staying calm. Keeping your emotions in check. I remember when my partner and I used to argue about chores. I'd get so worked up, you'd think we were debating world peace, not who should do the dishes. But here's what I learned: the moment you lose your cool, you've already lost the argument.

Try this instead: Take a deep breath. Count to ten if you need to. Then, instead of unleashing your frustration, say something like, 'I've noticed we both get pretty frustrated about chores. How about we sit down and figure out a way to divide them that feels fair for both of us?' See the difference? You're addressing the issue without turning it into World War III.

Next up: focus on the issue, not the person. When we're feeling defensive, it's so easy to start throwing personal jabs. But attacking the person just puts them on the defensive and gets you nowhere. Instead, try focusing on the specific behavior that's bothering you. For example, if your friend keeps canceling plans last minute, instead of saying, 'You're so inconsiderate,' try, 'When you cancel plans at the last minute, it makes me feel like my time isn't valued.' You're addressing the issue without making it a personal attack.

Now, here we have seeking solutions together. We often think that our solution is obviously the best one but, when you work together to find a solution, magic happens. Not only do you solve the problem, but you also strengthen your relationship.

And here's the kicker: apologizing. Admitting we're wrong can feel like pulling teeth. But a sincere apology can work wonders. For example, if you missed an important meeting with a friend, you might say, "I'm really sorry I missed our meeting. I understand if you're upset, and I want to make it up to you". It's not about groveling or losing face. It's about taking responsibility and showing that you value the relationship more than your ego.

Next time you find yourself in a conflict, try these techniques. Stay calm, focus on the issue, seek solutions together, and be ready to apologize if needed. It's not about winning the battle. It's about strengthening your relationships and creating a more positive environment around you.

I'm not gonna lie, it's not always easy. But every time I manage to approach a conflict with empathy, it turns out better. My relationships are stronger, problems actually get solved, and I feel pretty damn good about myself too.

Exercises to Develop Empathy

Empathy is not just an abstract concept but a practical skill that can be applied in everyday life. That is why developing it is totally possible. It's kind of like working out a muscle – the more you use it, the stronger it gets. Just like learning any new skill, it takes some practice and effort, but it's worth it.

Consider this: Our brains are pretty amazing. They can change and adapt, even as adults. Scientists call this "neuroplasticity." It's a fancy way of saying our brains can form new connections. So when we practice empathy, we're actually rewiring our brains to be better at it. This means that with consistent practice, we can strengthen the neural pathways associated with empathy, making it a more natural and automatic response.

Now, how do we actually get better at empathy? There are a bunch of ways:

Mindfulness Practices.

- **Mindful Listening** involves fully focusing on the speaker without interrupting or planning your response while they are talking. This practice helps you understand the speaker's emotions and perspectives more deeply.

  How to Practice: During conversations, make a conscious effort to listen without judgment. Pay attention to the speaker's words, tone, and body language. Reflect back what you've heard to ensure you understand their message accurately.

- **Mindful Observation** entails observing others in a non-judgmental way, paying close attention to their expressions, behaviors, and interactions.

  How to Practice: Spend time in a public place, like a park or café, and observe people around you. Notice their body language, facial expressions, and interactions. Try to infer what they might be feeling based on these observations without jumping to conclusions.

Perspective-Taking Activities

- **Role-Playing Scenarios** involve acting out situations from another person's perspective to understand their thoughts and feelings.

  How to Practice: In a group setting, take turns role-playing different scenarios where one person faces a challenge or conflict. Try to genuinely adopt the role of the other person and express their feelings and reactions. Discuss the experience afterward to gain insights into each other's perspectives.

- **Writing Exercises,** such as writing from another person's point of view, help develop cognitive empathy by imagining what it's like to be in someone else's shoes.

  How to Practice: Choose a person you interact with regularly and write a journal entry from their perspective. Consider their daily challenges, emotions, and thoughts. Reflect on how this exercise changes your understanding of their experiences and behaviors.

Empathy-Building Games.

- **Empathy Card Games** are designed to facilitate discussions and reflections on various emotions and scenarios, helping players develop a deeper understanding of others' feelings.

  How to Practice: Use commercially available empathy card games or create your own. Each card can describe a situation or emotion, and players take turns drawing cards and discussing how they would feel and react in those situations. This helps build emotional awareness and understanding.

- **Interactive Group Activities,** such as team-building exercises or cooperative games, encourage collaboration and perspective-taking.

  How to Practice: Participate in group activities that require teamwork and communication. For example, in a trust-building exercise, partners must rely on each other to complete a task. Reflect on how these activities help you understand and empathize with your teammates' experiences and perspectives.

Reflective Practices.

- **Daily Reflection Prompts** encourage you to think about your interactions and how you responded to others' emotions and needs.

  How to Practice: At the end of each day, spend a few minutes reflecting on your interactions. Use prompts such as, "Did I listen actively to someone today?" or "How did I show empathy in my interactions?" Write down your reflections to track your progress over time.

- **Empathy Journals** provide a dedicated space to record your thoughts and reflections on your empathetic experiences and growth.

How to Practice: Keep a journal where you regularly write about situations where you practiced empathy. Reflect on how you felt, what you learned, and how you can improve. This practice helps reinforce your empathetic behaviors and track your development.

Empathy in Action.

- **Volunteer Work** allows you to connect with people from different backgrounds and understand their challenges and needs.

  How to Practice: Choose a volunteer opportunity that interests you, such as working at a food bank, animal shelter, or community center. Engage with the people you are helping, listen to their stories, and reflect on their experiences. Volunteering provides firsthand experience in understanding and addressing the needs of others.

- **Random Acts of Kindness** involve doing something thoughtful for others without expecting anything in return, fostering empathy and compassion.

  How to Practice: Look for opportunities to perform small acts of kindness in your daily life, such as helping a neighbor with groceries, complimenting a coworker, or leaving a positive note for someone. Reflect on how these actions make you feel and how they impact the recipient. These acts help build a habit of empathy and altruism.

Daily Practices for Cultivating Empathy

1. Spend quality time with family members and engage in conversations about their experiences and feelings. Show interest in their daily lives and offer support during difficult times. Recognize and respect each family member's unique perspective and emotional needs.

2. In romantic relationships, prioritize open and honest communication. Listen to your partner's concerns and feelings without judgment. Express empathy by acknowledging their emotions and offering comfort and support. Regularly check in with your partner to understand their needs and how you can help meet them.

3. In friendships, practice active listening and validation. Show appreciation and support for your friends' achievements and challenges. Be present during conversations and offer a non-judgmental space for them to share their feelings.

4. At work, practice active listening with colleagues and employees. Understand their perspectives and concerns, and respond with empathy. Show appreciation for their contributions and provide constructive feedback in a supportive manner.

5. In customer service roles, listen to customers' concerns attentively. Acknowledge their frustrations and show understanding by saying things like, "I understand how frustrating this must be for you." Offer solutions in a calm and supportive tone.

6. During conflicts, practice active listening to understand each party's viewpoint. Validate their feelings and work towards a solution that addresses their concerns. Maintain a calm and respectful demeanor to create a collaborative environment for resolving issues.

7. When communicating online, use clear and considerate language. Pay attention to the tone of your messages and avoid misunderstandings by being explicit about your intentions. Respond thoughtfully to others' posts and comments, showing understanding and support.

8. Engage with others on social media by liking, sharing, and commenting on their posts in a supportive manner. Avoid negative or inflammatory comments. Respect differing opinions and respond with kindness, even in disagreements.

EMOTIONAL STABILITY

Emotions play a powerful role in shaping your thoughts and behaviors and they can be such a rollercoaster. It's not just about being moody - there's a whole lot going on under the surface and it's a tough cycle to break, but understanding where it all comes from is the first step.

Let's break this down and really get into how our emotions are pulling the strings in our daily lives. It's like being the director of your own movie - once you understand what's going on behind the scenes, you can start calling the shots instead of just reacting.

Emotional Triggers

Emotions often act as triggers for specific thoughts and behaviors....like hidden landmines in your day. Maybe it's a certain tone of voice that sets you off, or a situation that makes you feel small. The key is to start noticing these triggers. When you feel that surge of emotion, pause and ask yourself, "What just happened? What am I really reacting to here?"

Journaling Prompt:

- *Write down specific instances when you felt a strong emotional response. What were you doing? Who were you with? What was said or done that triggered your reaction?*
- *Look for patterns in your journal entries. Are there common themes or situations that repeatedly trigger your emotions?*
- *Try to understand why these situations trigger such strong emotions. Often, these triggers are linked to past experiences or unresolved issues.*

Behavioral Responses

Next, let's talk about how feelings drive actions. It's like emotions are the engine, and your behaviors are the car. When you're angry, you might lash out. When you're insecure, you might try to show off. Start paying attention to this connection. Ask yourself, "How is this feeling influencing what I'm about to do?"

Journaling Prompt:

- *Reflect on a recent situation where you felt a strong emotional response and reacted impulsively. What was the situation, who was involved, and how did you respond? How do you feel about your reaction now, and what could you have done differently?*

- *Think about a time when you felt validated or admired. How did you behave towards others in that situation? Contrast this with a time when you felt criticized or slighted—how did your behavior differ? What patterns do you notice in these contrasting scenarios?*
- *Describe a moment when you felt intense anger or frustration. What thoughts were going through your mind, and how did these thoughts drive your actions? Consider how recognizing and challenging these thoughts could alter your response in similar situations.*

Cognitive Distortions

These are the funhouse mirrors of your mind. They warp your perception of reality. Maybe you always jump to the worst-case scenario, or you think in all-or-nothing terms. Learning to spot these distortions is like putting on a pair of reality-check glasses.

Journaling Prompt:

- *Recall a recent social event where you felt out of place or insecure. Write about the thoughts that went through your mind and how they influenced your behavior. Were these thoughts based on evidence, or could they be cognitive distortions?*
- *Reflect on a time when you perceived yourself as a victim of unjust treatment. Describe the situation in detail. Were there alternative ways to interpret the feedback or actions of others? How might you reframe this experience to foster a more balanced perspective?*
- *Think about a recent instance when you felt validated and important. How did this affect your perception of yourself and your interactions with others? Consider whether your thoughts leaned towards grandiosity and how you can maintain a realistic self-view.*

Impact on Decision-Making

And don't forget about how strong emotions can hijack your decision-making. When you're riding high on excitement or drowning in anxiety, your choices might not be the best. It's like trying to drive through a storm - your vision is clouded.

Journaling Prompt:

- *Describe a situation where strong emotions led you to make an impulsive decision that you later regretted. What were the emotions, and what was the decision? Reflect on how recognizing your emotional state earlier might have changed the outcome.*
- *Write about a time when you felt extremely angry and were tempted to react harshly, such as sending a confrontational email or message. How did you handle the situation? If you acted impulsively, what were the consequences, and how could you have managed your emotions to make a better decision?*
- *Think about a major decision you made when you were feeling particularly emotional, whether it was anger, excitement, or fear. How did your emotional state influence your decision-making process? What strategies can you implement to ensure more balanced and rational decisions in the future?*

The goal here is to create a little space between your emotions and your actions. It's not about suppressing your feelings - it's about understanding them so they don't run the show.

Start small. Maybe next time you feel that surge of anger, take a deep breath before you respond. Or when you're about to make a big decision, check in with yourself: "Am I in the right headspace for this?"

Remember, this is a skill, and like any skill, it takes practice. You'll mess up sometimes, and that's okay. The important thing is to keep at it. Over time, you'll start to see patterns, and you'll get better at catching yourself before you react.

By doing this work, you're not just improving your own life - you're changing how you interact with everyone around you. It's like dropping a pebble in a pond - the ripples spread out and affect everything.

So give it a shot. Pay attention to your emotions, question your thoughts, and make decisions from a place of awareness rather than knee-jerk reactions.

Recognizing and Understanding Your Emotions

You know the drill - your self-esteem's like a house of cards, you're always chasing that next hit of validation, and your coping mechanisms? Well, let's just say they could use some work.

Here's the thing - a lot of us with these traits? We're not exactly in touch with our feelings. It's like we're emotionally colorblind. We might think we're feeling one thing, but it's actually something completely different. And don't even get me started on understanding other people's emotions. It's like trying to read a book in a language we never learned.

But here's the good news - we can learn this language. It starts with recognizing that our emotional instability is often because we're not processing our feelings properly. It's like we've got all these unacknowledged emotions bubbling under the surface, and they're just waiting to explode.

First, we've got to start paying attention. Next time you find yourself blowing up at someone, take a step back. Ask yourself, "What am I really feeling here?" Maybe you're not actually angry - maybe you're feeling hurt, or scared, or embarrassed.

But developing emotional awareness isn't just about thinking - it's about doing. Here are some exercises that can really help you get in touch with your feelings:

1. **Pause and Reflect:** Throughout your day, hit the pause button. Ask yourself, "What am I feeling right now?" Is it happiness, sadness, anxiety, anger? Don't judge it, just notice it. It's like taking a snapshot of your emotional state.
2. **Body Scan:** Our bodies often know what we're feeling before our brains do. Try

this - close your eyes and mentally scan your body from head to toe. Notice any tension, any sensations. That tightness in your chest? It might be anxiety. That warmth in your cheeks? Could be embarrassment.

3. **Name That Emotion:** When you feel something strongly, try to give it a specific name. Instead of just "bad," is it disappointment? Frustration? The more precise you can be, the better you'll understand yourself.

4. **Emotion Journal:** At the end of each day, jot down the emotions you experienced. What triggered them? How did you react? Over time, you'll start to see patterns.

5. **Mindfulness Meditation:** Spend just five minutes a day sitting quietly, focusing on your breath. When thoughts or feelings come up, notice them without judgment. It's like training your brain to observe your emotions.

6. **Empathy Practice:** When you're talking with someone, really try to imagine how they're feeling. It's not about fixing their problems - just understanding. This can help you get better at recognizing emotions in yourself too.

7. **The "Why" Chain:** When you feel something strongly, ask yourself why. Then ask why again. Keep going. You might be surprised at what you uncover.

This isn't about changing your emotions or judging them. It's about becoming aware of them. It's like turning on a light in a dark room - suddenly you can see what's really there.

Start small. Maybe try one of these exercises each day. But stick with it. The more you practice, the more natural it'll become.

And here's the cool part - as you get better at recognizing and understanding your emotions, you'll likely find that you're less reactive. You'll have more control over your responses. Your relationships might improve. You might even feel more at peace with yourself.

Understanding Rage and Anger

For folks with narcissistic traits, anger and rage can be particularly intense and frequent. Here's the deal: for us, anger often pops up when we feel like our self-esteem is under attack. It could be something as simple as someone else getting praised at work. Suddenly, we're thinking, "What the hell? I'm the star here!" And before we know it, we're seething inside. Or maybe your partner tries to give you some feedback. Instead of hearing it as helpful, it feels like a full-on assault. "How dare they criticize me?" we think. And boom - we're on the defensive, maybe even lashing out. Even in social situations, if we're not getting the attention we crave, it can spark this anger. We might start interrupting people or bragging about ourselves just to get the spotlight back.

The problem is, these reactions? They're like relationship poison. We end up pushing people away, straining our work relationships, and feeling even more isolated and misunderstood.

But here's the thing - we can change this pattern. It starts with recognizing what's really going on. Next time you feel that anger bubbling up, try to hit pause for a second. Ask yourself:

1. *What's really triggering this? Is it actually a threat, or am I just perceiving it that way?*
2. *Is this anger proportional to the situation?*
3. *What am I really feeling underneath the anger? Hurt? Insecure? Scared?*

Just being aware of these patterns is a huge first step. Maybe next time a colleague gets praised, instead of getting angry, you could try genuinely congratulating them. Or when your partner gives feedback, take a deep breath and try to listen without immediately getting defensive.

Anger Management Techniques

Managing anger involves both immediate techniques to calm yourself in the moment and long-term strategies to prevent anger from building up. Here are some effective anger management techniques tailored to those with narcissistic traits:

Breathing Exercises and Mindfulness: Deep breathing exercises can help calm your nervous system and reduce the intensity of your anger. Practice inhaling deeply through your nose, holding your breath for a few seconds, and exhaling slowly through your mouth. Mindfulness techniques, such as focusing on the present moment and observing your thoughts without judgment, can also help you gain control over your emotions. For individuals with narcissistic traits, mindfulness can help ground them and reduce the focus on perceived threats to their ego.

Cognitive Behavioral Strategies: Cognitive behavioral strategies involve changing the thought patterns that contribute to your anger. This can include identifying irrational thoughts and replacing them with more rational, balanced perspectives. For example, instead of thinking, "This criticism proves I'm a failure," you might reframe it as, "Everyone makes mistakes, and I can learn from this feedback."

Progressive Muscle Relaxation: Progressive muscle relaxation involves tensing and then slowly relaxing different muscle groups in your body. This technique can help release physical tension associated with anger and promote a sense of calm. Regular practice can help reduce the overall intensity of your anger responses.

Anger Journaling and Reflection: Keeping an anger journal can be a valuable tool for understanding your anger patterns. Write down the situations that triggered your anger, how you responded, and the consequences of your actions. Reflecting on these entries can help you identify patterns and develop better strategies for managing your anger. For those with narcissistic traits, journaling can also provide insights into how their anger affects their relationships and self-perception.

COMMON EMOTIONS & THEIR MEANINGS

Happiness

Meaning: A feeling of pleasure, contentment, or joy.

When: Achieving goals, spending time with loved ones, engaging in enjoyable activities.

How it Feels in the Body: Lightness in the chest, smiling, relaxed muscles.

Example: Feeling joyful when receiving good news or laughing with friends.

Sadness

Meaning: A feeling of sorrow, disappointment, or grief.

When: Experiencing loss, failure, or disappointment.

How it Feels in the Body: Heaviness in the chest, crying, slumped posture.

Example: Feeling heartbroken after a breakup or mourning the loss of a loved one.

Anger

Meaning: A feeling of strong displeasure or hostility.

When: Facing injustice, frustration, or perceived threats.

How it Feels in the Body: Tension in the body, clenched fists, increased heart rate.

Example: Feeling enraged when treated unfairly at work or during a heated argument.

Fear

Meaning: A feeling of anxiety or apprehension about potential danger or harm.

When: Facing a threat, unknown situations, or personal safety concerns.

How it Feels in the Body: Rapid heartbeat, sweating, shallow breathing.

Example: Feeling scared when speaking in public or during a dangerous situation.

Disgust

Meaning: A feeling of revulsion or strong disapproval.

When: Encountering something offensive, unpleasant, or morally wrong.

How it Feels in the Body: Nausea, wrinkling the nose, turning away.

Example: Feeling repulsed by a foul smell or witnessing unethical behavior.

Surprise

Meaning: A feeling of shock or astonishment, usually in response to an unexpected event.

When: Encountering something unexpected, whether positive or negative.

How it Feels in the Body: Raised eyebrows, widened eyes, open mouth.

Example: Feeling startled by a sudden loud noise or pleasantly surprised by an unexpected gift.

COMMON EMOTIONS & THEIR MEANINGS

Love

Meaning: A deep affection or attachment towards someone or something.

When: Experiencing closeness, intimacy, or strong connection.

How it Feels in the Body: Warmth in the chest, calmness, desire for physical closeness.

Example: Feeling affectionate towards a partner or deep appreciation for a close friend.

Guilt

Meaning: A feeling of remorse or regret for a wrongdoing.

When: Realizing you have hurt someone or violated personal or societal standards.

How it Feels in the Body: Heaviness in the stomach, unease, avoidance of eye contact.

Example: Feeling guilty after lying to a friend or failing to fulfill a promise.

Shame

Meaning: A feeling of humiliation or distress due to perceived wrong behavior or inadequacy.

When: Experiencing failure, rejection, or social disapproval.

How it Feels in the Body: Blushing, sinking feeling in the stomach, avoiding others.

Example: Feeling ashamed after making a public mistake or being criticized.

Jealousy

Meaning: A feeling of envy towards someone else's advantages or possessions.

When: Comparing oneself unfavorably to others, fearing loss of affection or status.

How it Feels in the Body: Tension in the chest, restlessness, negative thoughts.

Example: Feeling jealous when a partner gives attention to someone else or a colleague gets a promotion.

Embarrassment

Meaning: A feeling of awkwardness or self-consciousness.

When: Being the center of unwanted attention, making a mistake in public.

How it Feels in the Body: Blushing, sweating, nervous laughter.

Example: Feeling embarrassed after tripping in front of a crowd or forgetting someone's name.

Contentment

Meaning: A state of satisfaction and peace.

When: Enjoying the present moment, feeling at ease with life.

How it Feels in the Body: Relaxed muscles, calm breathing, gentle smile.

Example: Feeling content while enjoying a quiet evening at home or after completing

Long-Term Anger Management

In addition to immediate techniques, long-term strategies are essential for maintaining emotional stability and preventing anger from becoming a chronic issue.

Developing Healthy Outlets for Anger: Finding healthy ways to express your anger can prevent it from building up and leading to rage. This might include engaging in creative activities like art or music, participating in sports, or finding a hobby that allows you to channel your emotions constructively. For individuals with narcissistic traits, these outlets can also provide a sense of achievement and self-worth that is not reliant on external validation.

Building Empathy and Understanding: Empathy involves understanding and sharing the feelings of others. By building empathy, you can improve your relationships and reduce conflicts that might trigger anger. Practice active listening and try to see situations from others' perspectives. For those with narcissistic traits, developing empathy can be a significant step towards reducing self-centered behaviors and fostering healthier relationships.

Regular Physical Exercise: Regular physical exercise is a powerful tool for managing anger. Exercise releases endorphins, which can improve your mood and reduce stress. Activities like running, swimming, or yoga can help you release pent-up energy and tension. For individuals with narcissistic traits, exercise can also be a way to build discipline and resilience.

Establishing Support Networks: Having a strong support network of friends, family, or support groups can provide emotional support and guidance when you're feeling angry. Talking to someone you trust about your feelings can help you process your emotions and find constructive ways to deal with them. For those with narcissistic traits, supportive relationships can also provide validation and encouragement in a healthy way.

Regular Physical Activity and Healthy Lifestyle: Physical activity is a powerful tool for managing emotions. Regular exercise releases endorphins, which can improve mood and reduce stress. Maintaining a healthy lifestyle, including a balanced diet and sufficient sleep, also supports emotional well-being and resilience.

Practicing Gratitude and Positive Thinking: Practicing gratitude involves regularly reflecting on and appreciating the positive aspects of your life. This practice can shift your focus away from negative thoughts and reduce emotional volatility. Positive thinking, such as reframing challenges as opportunities for growth, can also enhance emotional resilience.

IMPROVING RELATIONSHIPS

If you're anything like me, you've probably found relationships to be a bit of a minefield. That's okay – it's a common struggle. Why? Well, it's a perfect storm of factors: maybe you're not always tuned in to your own behavior, or you find it tough to put yourself in someone else's shoes. Perhaps you've got a complicated relationship with honesty, or you struggle to show respect consistently. And let's be real – maintaining connections takes work, something that might not always be your strong suit.

Understanding these challenges is the first step to overcoming them. Now, I'm not saying it's going to be a walk in the park. Building healthier, more fulfilling relationships takes effort, self-awareness, and a genuine commitment to personal growth. But let me tell you, it's worth it. Imagine having a network of supportive, loving relationships. Sounds pretty good, right?

Let's dig into a scenario that might feel familiar. Picture this: you've got two people in a relationship – let's call them Mark and Jane. Mark's the one with narcissistic traits (sound like anyone you know?), while Jane doesn't share those tendencies.

Jane often feels like she's tiptoeing around Mark, afraid to say the wrong thing. She notices that no matter what they're talking about, the conversation always circles back to Mark's achievements or problems. When she tries to express her own needs, Mark either brushes them off or gets defensive, leaving Jane feeling guilty for even bringing them up.

On the flip side, Mark (and maybe you can relate to this) feels like Jane doesn't appreciate everything he brings to the table. When Jane asks for more emotional support, it feels like a personal attack. He's trying his best – why can't she see that? He's constantly looking for affirmation, and when he doesn't get it, he either lashes out or retreats.

Familiar territory? I thought it might be. But don't worry – recognizing this dynamic is a huge step forward. In the next section, we'll talk about how to improve this situation, and I've got some strategies that can help you navigate these waters and build stronger, more fulfilling relationships.

Building and Maintaining Healthy Relationships

Building and maintaining healthy relationships isn't about grand romantic gestures or flashy displays of affection. It's about the small stuff - the day-in, day-out effort to genuinely connect with people. So, where do we start? It all begins with you.

Self-Awareness: You've got to get to know yourself and be present. And I mean really know yourself. It's time for some honest self-reflection. Ask yourself, "How do my words and actions affect the people around me?" Don't worry if the answers aren't all sunshine and roses. We're here to learn about ourselves, and the more self-aware you become, the better equipped you are to build those deep, meaningful connections we all crave.

Everything we've discussed ultimately boils down to self-awareness. Without it, we can't truly understand how our behaviors impact others or why we react the way we do. Self-awareness is the foundation upon which empathy, communication, and relationship-building are built.

We often see the world through our own unique lens, which can distort our perceptions. I remember a time when I kept interrupting my partner during conversations. In my mind, I was just eager to share my brilliant insights. It took me a while to realize that what I saw as enthusiasm, they experienced as disrespect. Talk about a wake-up call!

Real-Life Examples:

- You frequently interrupt others during conversations, believing your input is more important, and not realizing how this frustrates others.
- In social settings, you monopolize the conversation, leaving little room for others to share their thoughts, making them feel undervalued.
- When colleagues provide constructive criticism, you dismiss it outright, thinking they don't understand your approach.
- You react defensively to any form of critique, often blaming others instead of reflecting on your own actions.
- You fail to notice when people around you seem uncomfortable or hurt by your comments or jokes.
- You rarely apologize for your actions, believing that you are always right.
- You consistently blame others for any failures or mistakes in collaborative projects, avoiding any personal responsibility.
- You do not spend time reflecting on your actions and their impacts, leading to repeated negative behaviors.

Ways to Improve:

1. Keep a daily journal to reflect on your interactions. Write down what happened, how you reacted, and how it might have affected others.
2. A therapist can help you identify patterns and provide guidance for change offering outside neutral perspective on your behaviors.
3. Ask friends or family for honest feedback about your behavior and be open to their insights.

Honesty: Honesty is like the foundation of a house. Without it, the whole structure can come crumbling down. And I'm not just talking about avoiding lies (though that's important too). I'm talking about real, raw transparency—sharing your true thoughts and feelings, even when it's tough.

For example, if something bothers you in your relationship, address it honestly rather than bottling it up. Transparency prevents a whole lot of drama down the line. Plus, it gives the other person a chance to actually address the issue. Who knows? Maybe they didn't even realize it was bothering you.

Honesty can feel... well, kinda scary. Why? We often feel the need to maintain a certain image. We want to appear perfect, infallible, always in control. The thought of admitting a mistake or showing vulnerability? That can feel like kryptonite. We do it to impress others, to feed that need for admiration. But here's the kicker: it actually pushes people away in the long run.

Nobody's perfect. We all make mistakes; we all have flaws. Admitting them doesn't make you weak—it makes you human. And in my experience, people connect a lot more with humans than with perfectly polished facades.

Real-Life Examples:

- You frequently embellish your accomplishments to impress others, even if it means stretching the truth.
- When you make a mistake at work, you cover it up instead of admitting it and learning from it.
- You selectively share information to manipulate others into seeing you in a better light.
- You avoid discussing important issues in your relationships, leading to unresolved conflicts and misunderstandings.
- You consistently shift blame onto others to avoid taking responsibility for your actions.
- You lie about your intentions or plans to avoid confrontation or to gain favor.
- You keep your true feelings hidden, creating a barrier to genuine connection.
- You engage in behaviors that you hide from others, such as financial mismanagement or infidelity.
- You pretend to agree with others to avoid conflict, even if you have no intention of following through.

Ways to Improve:

1. Make a conscious effort to be truthful in your interactions. Start with small steps, like being honest about your weekend activities, and build up to more significant issues.
2. Practice being vulnerable by sharing your true thoughts and feelings, even if it feels uncomfortable. Vulnerability can strengthen relationships by showing that you trust the other person.
3. Hold yourself accountable for your words and actions. If you make a mistake, admit it and work to make amends. This might involve saying, "I was wrong, and I'm sorry for how I acted."

Mutual Respect: So, what does real respect look like in relationships? It's about truly valuing the other person's perspective, even if it's miles away from your own.

Let me paint you a picture. You're in a heated debate with your partner about, I don't know, whether pineapple belongs on pizza (it doesn't, by the way - but that's beside the point). Your first instinct might be to steamroll over their opinion and prove why you're right. Been there, done that.

But what if we tried something different? What if, before launching into your ironclad argument, you took a moment to really hear them out? Saying something like, "I see where you're coming from. That's an interesting point," sounds simple, right? But let me tell you, this little shift can be revolutionary.

Why it's tough? We often carry around this sense that we're... well, better. Smarter. More important. So, when someone disagrees with us or sets a boundary, it can feel like a personal attack. This makes it difficult to truly respect others' perspectives, but learning to do so can drastically improve your relationships.

Real-Life Examples

- During meetings, you interrupt others and dismiss their ideas without consideration.
- You frequently invade others' personal space or time without respecting their boundaries.
- You take credit for others' work or ideas, believing you are more deserving of recognition.
- You fail to acknowledge or appreciate the contributions of team members, undermining their efforts.
- You make derogatory comments about others' abilities or ideas, diminishing their confidence and contributions.
- You make decisions that affect others without consulting them, disregarding their input or preferences.
- In conflicts, you refuse to find middle ground, insisting that your way is the only correct way.
- You expect special treatment and become upset when others do not cater to your demands.
- You undermine the authority of leaders or peers, believing you know better.
- You use dismissive language or tone when others express their views, making them feel undervalued.

Ways to Improve:

1. Make a habit of acknowledging and appreciating different viewpoints and contributions. For example, say, "I see where you're coming from, and I think your perspective is valuable."
2. Learn to recognize and respect others' boundaries. Ask for consent and ensure you are not imposing on others. This might involve asking, "Is it okay if we discuss this now, or would another time be better for you?"

3. Strive to treat relationships as equal partnerships, valuing the input and needs of others as much as your own. This means making decisions together and ensuring everyone's voice is heard.

Consistent Effort: Relationships thrive on consistent effort. They are like plants; you can't just water them once and expect them to thrive. They need regular TLC to grow and flourish. And I'm not talking about grand gestures or over-the-top displays of affection (though those can be nice too). I'm talking about the small, everyday stuff that shows people you care.

If you're anything like I used to be, consistency might not be your strong suit. For those of us with narcissistic tendencies, it can be a real challenge. Why? Well, we tend to be pretty focused on our own needs and wants. We might make a big splash with grand gestures—surprise parties, expensive gifts—but struggle with the day-to-day nurturing that relationships need.

Real-Life Examples

- You reach out to friends or family sporadically, often only when you need something, making others feel used.
- You frequently forget birthdays, anniversaries, or other significant events, showing a lack of attention to others' lives.
- You often cancel plans at the last minute for personal convenience, disregarding others' schedules and feelings.
- You make promises or commitments that you do not follow through on, leading others to see you as unreliable.
- You expect others to initiate contact and make efforts to maintain the relationship while you contribute little effort.
- You rarely express gratitude or appreciation for others' actions, taking their efforts for granted.
- Your interactions remain surface-level, avoiding deeper, meaningful conversations or connections.
- You fail to recognize or reciprocate small acts of kindness, which can make relationships feel unbalanced.
- You consistently prioritize your own needs and desires over those of others, leading to feelings of neglect or resentment.
- You seldom check in on friends or family to see how they are doing, missing opportunities to show you care.

Ways to Improve:

1. Make a habit of regularly checking in with friends and loved ones. Put reminders in your calendar if needed. A simple, "How are you doing?" can go a long way.
2. Remember important dates and celebrate milestones with others. This shows that you care and value their presence in your life. For example, send a card or a message

on birthdays and anniversaries.

3.   Dedicate quality time to your relationships. Engage in activities that your friends and family enjoy and show interest in their lives. Plan regular outings or simple activities like having a meal together.
4.   Regularly express your appreciation for others' efforts and presence in your life. A simple "thank you" can strengthen bonds.
5.   Follow through on commitments and promises. Consistency builds trust and shows that you value the relationship.

How to Rebuilding Trust

It's time to tackle the elephant in the room: rebuilding trust. If you're anything like I was, you might have left a trail of strained or broken relationships in your wake. When you've been treating people with those classic narcissistic behaviors—you know, the manipulation, the dishonesty, the 'it's all about me' attitude—trust can crumble faster than a sandcastle at high tide.

But all hope isn't lost. Trust can be rebuilt. Is it easy? Hell no. Is it worth it? Absolutely.

Now, this journey is uncomfortable. It's painful. It involves breaking through those defense mechanisms that protect our fragile self-esteem, admitting our flaws and wrongdoings. It feels like an attack on one's very identity, and accepting that you have hurt others requires a level of humility and vulnerability that can be profoundly unsettling. For example, if you have consistently manipulated friends or family members to get your way, admitting that you were wrong can shake you to the core.

But that discomfort is where the growth happens. It's like working out—if it doesn't challenge you, it doesn't change you.

Next up: growing beyond that ego of ours. It's about shifting from 'me, me, me' to 'us, us, us'. It's learning to find value in yourself without needing constant validation from others. It's understanding that considering others' needs doesn't diminish your own worth. It's about embracing humility by accepting that you are not perfect and that it's okay to make mistakes. It involves developing empathy by actively trying to understand and share the feelings of others. It's about taking full responsibility for your actions without making excuses or shifting blame.

Let's break it down into actionable steps that we can follow to rebuild trust in a meaningful way.

Step 1: Owning Up to Our Mess

First things first: we've got to face the music. Admitting we messed up isn't exactly our strong suit, but it's the foundation of everything else we're going to do. Think back to those moments when you let your narcissistic tendencies run wild. Maybe you constantly hogged the spotlight, leaving your friend feeling invisible. Or perhaps you dismissed your partner's feelings because they didn't align with yours. It's time to shine a light on those moments.

Here's what I want you to do: Sit down and make a list of specific incidents where you know you hurt someone. Then, take a deep breath and say it out loud: "I messed up." No ifs, ands, or buts. No "I'm sorry you felt that way." Just a straight-up acknowledgment of your actions and their impact.

Step 2: Let's Talk (And Actually Listen)

Now that we've ripped off the Band-Aid, it's time to open up those lines of communication. And when I say open, I mean wide open. This is where it gets tricky for us. We're used to dominating conversations, right? Well, it's time to flip the script. Your job now is to listen. Really listen. Not just waiting for your turn to speak, but actually trying to understand where the other person is coming from.

When they're talking, resist the urge to get defensive. Instead, try reflecting back what you're hearing. "So, what I'm understanding is that when I did X, you felt Y. Is that right?" And when it's your turn to share, be honest about your feelings, but remember - this isn't about making excuses. It's about understanding and healing.

Step 3: Walk the Walk

Here's where the rubber meets the road. We've talked the talk, now it's time to walk the walk. Consistently. It's time to keep all those promises you made. Every. Single. One. I know it's tempting to fall back into old patterns, but resist that urge. Every time you follow through on a commitment, you're laying another brick in the foundation of trust.

Set up routines and stick to them. Be present in your relationships. Show up not just physically, but emotionally too. It might feel awkward at first, like you're trying to write with your non-dominant hand. But keep at it. It gets easier.

Step 4: Sorry Seems to be the Hardest Word

Not those half-hearted "sorry if you were offended" non-apologies. I'm talking about genuine, heartfelt "I messed up and I'm truly sorry" apologies. Be specific about what you're sorry for. "I'm sorry for always putting my needs first and ignoring yours." Acknowledge the hurt you caused. "I understand that my actions made you feel unimportant and unloved." And most importantly, talk about how you're going to do better. "I'm working on being more attentive and considerate, and here's how..."

Step 5: Patience is a Virtue (That We Need to Learn)

After all this hard work, you don't get an immediate gold star and everything isn't magically fixed. Rebuilding trust takes time. Sometimes a lot of time. This is where our patience gets tested. We're used to instant gratification. Well, this isn't that. You've got to keep putting in the work, day after day, even when it feels like you're not making progress. There will be setbacks. The person you hurt might lash out or express doubt. When that happens, take a deep breath and respond with empathy, not defensiveness. Remember, their healing process is just as important as your growth.

Understanding and Addressing Jealousy

Jealousy is a tricky beast. It's like a toxic cocktail of insecurity, fear, and anxiety, all wrapped up in the fear of losing something we value - whether that's a relationship, status, or admiration from others.

Jealousy often boils down to the fear of being outshined or losing that precious validation we crave. It's like we're constantly on guard, worried someone might steal our spotlight. Now, this jealousy can show up in some pretty ugly ways. We might find ourselves criticizing others, trying to undermine their success. It's like we're thinking, "If I can't be the best, I'll make sure no one else looks good either." Or we might withdraw, isolating ourselves to protect our fragile ego from perceived threats.

In relationships, our jealousy can turn into possessiveness and control. We're so afraid of losing our source of admiration that we try to micromanage our partner's every move. It's not healthy, and it certainly doesn't build trust. We might even sabotage ourselves, subconsciously ensuring we don't succeed to avoid the pressure of maintaining that success. It's a twisted way our insecurities play out.

First, we've got to challenge our misconceptions about jealousy. It's not a sign of strength or justified entitlement. It's a signal that we need to work on our self-esteem and trust issues.

So, how do we tackle this green-eyed monster?

1. **Acknowledge It:** Admit it - we're jealous. It's not easy, but it's the first step.
2. **Shift Our Perspective:** Instead of seeing others' success as a threat, let's try to see it as inspiration. What can we learn from them?
3. **Practice Gratitude:** Focus on your own strengths and achievements. Keep a gratitude journal if it helps. Remind yourself of your worth that isn't dependent on being "better" than others.
4. **Communicate: Communication** is key, especially in relationships. If you're feeling jealous, talk about it openly. It's vulnerable, but it's so much better than letting those feelings fester.
5. **Build Genuine Self-Confidence:** Work on building genuine self-confidence. Not the kind that needs constant external validation, but the kind that comes from within.

Changing these patterns takes time and effort. But I promise you, you're not doomed to be jealous forever. You can learn to appreciate others without feeling threatened. You can build relationships based on trust instead of fear.

Integrity & Ethical Decision Making

Let's talk about integrity. It's more than just a fancy word—it's about living your life in a way that matches your values. It means being honest, reliable, and consistent in your actions. When you've got integrity, people know they can count on you to do the right thing, even when no one's watching.

This might feel like a real challenge. I get it. The temptation to exaggerate your achievements or take credit for others' work can be strong. That need for admiration and validation can sometimes overshadow your ethical compass. Let me give you a real-world example. Imagine you're part of a successful project at work. It's tempting to play up your role, right? To make it sound like you were the driving force behind the whole thing. But here's what integrity looks like in action: You say something like, "Our team worked really hard on this project, and I'm proud of the part I played. But it was definitely a group effort." See the difference? You're still acknowledging your contribution, but you're also giving credit where it's due.

Let's see how to build integrity:

1. **Start by taking a good, hard look at yourself.** Regularly check in on your actions and decisions. Ask yourself, "Would I be comfortable if everyone knew about this?" It's a simple question, but it can be a powerful guide.

2. **If you mess up—and we all do sometimes—own it.** Admit your mistake and take responsibility. It might feel uncomfortable in the moment, but it builds trust and shows others that you're committed to doing the right thing.

3. **Consistency is key.** Make sure your actions line up with your values, even when it's tough. It's easy to have integrity when everything's smooth sailing. The real test comes when you're faced with a difficult choice.

4. **Be open and honest in your dealings with others.** Resist the urge to hide information or manipulate situations to your advantage. It might seem like you're giving up an edge, but the trust and respect you gain are worth so much more.

Ethical decision-making is all about making choices that align with your values and moral standards. It's not just about what's good for you but considering how your decisions impact others. Let's break this down with a real-world example.

Imagine you've got access to some confidential info that could give you an edge in a business deal. Sure, using it might benefit you in the short term, but it would violate trust and confidentiality agreements. The ethical choice? Respect that confidentiality. You might say to yourself, "I can't use this information. It was shared in confidence, and respecting that trust is more important than any short-term gain."

It's easy to get caught up in what benefits you personally and overlook the bigger picture. But making ethical decisions isn't just good for others—it's good for you in the long run too.

So, how do you improve your ethical decision-making?

1. **Think About How Your Actions Will Affect Others,** Not Just Yourself. If you're faced with a choice that could impact your colleagues, take a step back and consider how it might play out for them.

2. **Don't Be Afraid to Seek out Other Perspectives.** Talk to people you trust, get their take on the situation. This is especially important if you tend to focus mainly on your own viewpoint. Other people might see angles you've missed.

3. **Try to Align Your Choices with Your Core Values.** What do you really believe in? Make sure your decisions reflect those principles. This helps you stay consistent and true to yourself.

4. **Think Long Terms.** It's easy to get caught up in immediate benefits, but consider the long-term implications of your choices. Will this decision still feel right a year from now? Five years from now?

By focusing on integrity and ethical decision-making, you can build stronger, more trustworthy relationships and create a life that truly reflects your values.

Showing Respect & Valuing Contributions

We're diving into the deep end of respect and how our narcissistic tendencies can sometimes make us... well, less than stellar in that department. Even if you are the smartest person in the room, acting with superiority and entitlement can make you the least likable person there. I've been there.

Let's paint a picture. You're in a meeting, and you've got this brilliant idea. So brilliant that you just can't wait for your colleague to finish their clearly inferior thought. So you jump in, cutting them off mid-sentence. Sound familiar? I used to think I was doing everyone a favor by sharing my genius ASAP.

Here's what I learned the hard way: respect isn't about agreeing with everyone or thinking their ideas are better than yours. It's about acknowledging that everyone has something valuable to contribute, even if it's just a different perspective.

Next time you're in a meeting and feel the urge to interrupt, try this instead: count to five, and actually listen to what your colleague is saying. When they're done, you could say something like, "That's an interesting point, Sarah. Building on that, I was thinking..." See what we did there? We acknowledged their contribution before adding our own.

Consider a personal relationship where you dismiss your partner's concerns during a discussion, making them feel unheard. Instead, you could validate their feelings by saying, "I understand that you're upset, and I want to hear more about what's bothering you." This approach shows empathy and respect, strengthening the emotional bond between you two.

By actively practicing respect and valuing others' contributions, you can create a more positive environment where everyone feels appreciated and acknowledged. This shift not only enhances your interactions but also helps you develop a more balanced and empathetic approach to others, fostering a healthier and more respectful environment in both personal and professional settings.

Let's talk about taking credit. I remember once, after a huge project, I stood up in front of the whole team and basically acted like I'd single-handedly saved the company. The looks on my teammates' faces? Let's just say they weren't planning my parade.

Here's the thing: acknowledging others doesn't diminish your own contribution. In fact, it makes you look even better. So next time, try this: "This project was a real team effort. I'm proud of what we accomplished together, and I couldn't have done it without Sarah's killer research skills and John's amazing design work."

And in our personal relationships? Oh man, this is where it really hits home. I can't tell you how many times I dismissed my partner's concerns because I thought they were overreacting.

Instead, try this on for size: When your partner brings up a concern, even if you think it's no big deal, take a moment to really hear them out. You could say, "I can see this is really bothering you. Can you tell me more about why you feel this way?" It's not about agreeing with everything they say. It's about showing them that their feelings matter to you.

Now, I'm not gonna lie. This shift might feel like you're giving up your power or admitting you're not as awesome as you thought. But true power comes from lifting others up, not pushing them down.

Improving respect and valuing contributions:

1. **Listen!!!!** Practice active listening by giving your full attention when someone else is speaking. This means not just hearing their words, but also understanding their message and showing that you value their input.

2. **Regularly Express Gratitude for Others' Efforts and Contributions.** Simple acknowledgments, like saying "thank you" or writing a note of appreciation, can go a long way in making others feel valued. For instance, if a friend helps you with a task, a heartfelt "I really appreciate your help" can strengthen your bond.

3. **Ensure that You Give Credit Where It's Due.** If you're working on a project with others, acknowledge their contributions openly. This builds trust and respect, showing that you value teamwork and collaboration. In a professional setting, you might say, "I couldn't have completed this project without [colleague's name]'s valuable insights and hard work."

4. **Encourage Others to Share Their Ideas and Opinions.** Create an environment where everyone feels comfortable contributing. This can be done by asking for input during discussions and validating their perspectives. For example, in a group discussion, ask quieter members for their thoughts and show appreciation for their contributions.

5. **Respect Personal Boundaries and Be Mindful Of Others' Comfort Levels.** This includes not imposing your views or demands on them. For instance, if a friend seems uncomfortable with a topic, steer the conversation in a different direction and respect their feelings.

HEALTHY ROMANTIC RELATIONSHIPS

Okay, let's talk about love. You know, that thing that's supposed to be all butterflies and rainbows but sometimes feels more like a minefield? Yeah, that's the one.

Now, for us, romantic relationships can be... let's just say 'challenging' is putting it mildly. It's like we're playing a game where we don't quite know the rules, and somehow, we keep accidentally setting the board on fire.

Let me paint you a picture. You're having a conversation with your partner. They're talking about their day, and you've got this brilliant story about your own day that you just can't wait to share. So you jump in, cutting them off mid-sentence. I used to do this all the time, thinking I was just being enthusiastic. Turns out, I was actually making my partner feel like their thoughts didn't matter.

Or how about this scenario: Your partner just got a promotion at work. Great news, right? But instead of celebrating with them, you find yourself saying something like, "Oh, that's nice. I remember when I got my first promotion..." And suddenly, their big moment becomes all about you. Oops.

And let's not forget the constant need for admiration. It's like we're emotional vampires, always needing that hit of validation. So we might flirt with others or constantly fish for compliments, not realizing we're creating a tsunami of insecurity and mistrust in our relationship.

Here's the thing: most of the time, we don't even realize we're doing these things! We're not trying to hurt our partners. We're just... being us. But that 'us' can be pretty toxic without some serious self-awareness and work.

I remember the day I realized how much damage I was doing. My partner sat me down and said, "I feel like I'm invisible in this relationship." It was like a bucket of ice water to the face. I thought I was being a great partner. After all, I was sharing all my amazing stories and achievements. So, so wrong.

But we can change this. We can build healthier, more fulfilling relationships.

Start by really listening to your partner. When they're sharing something, resist the urge to one-up them or turn the conversation back to you. Instead, try saying something like, "That sounds important to you. Can you tell me more about it?"

When your partner achieves something, celebrate their success without making it about you. A simple "That's awesome! I'm so proud of you" goes a long way.

And that need for constant admiration? Try to find ways to validate yourself instead of always seeking it from others. It's not easy, but it's so worth it.

A healthy relationship isn't about one person shining while the other stands in their shadow. It's about two people supporting each other, celebrating each other's successes, and growing together.

How To Validate Yourself

That constant need for admiration and validation can be overwhelming. It's like a never-ending hunger that can never be truly satisfied. But what if I told you that the key to breaking free from this cycle lies within you?

When you rely on others for validation, you give away your power. Your self-worth becomes dependent on external factors that you can't control. Learning to validate yourself gives you the power to define your own value and develop unshakable confidence. True confidence comes from within. It's about knowing and accepting yourself, flaws and all, and not needing constant external approval to feel good about who you are. Consequently, when you no longer need constant validation from others, your relationships become healthier. You can appreciate others for who they are without the pressure of seeking their approval. This fosters mutual respect and genuine connections.

Here are some practical strategies to help you validate yourself and build a healthier sense of self-worth:

Acknowledge Your Achievements: Take time to recognize your accomplishments, big and small. Keep a journal where you write down daily successes and things you're proud of. This helps build a positive self-image based on your own standards.

Set Personal Goals: Identify what you want to achieve for yourself, not for the approval of others. Set goals that align with your values and work towards them. Achieving these goals will bring you a sense of fulfillment that doesn't rely on external validation.

Practice Self-Compassion: Treat yourself with the same kindness and understanding you would offer a friend. When you make mistakes, don't beat yourself up. Instead, acknowledge your humanity and learn from the experience.

Positive Self-Talk: Be mindful of your inner dialogue. Replace self-critical thoughts with affirmations. For example, instead of thinking, "I'm not good enough," try telling yourself, "I'm learning and growing every day."

Celebrate Your Unique Qualities: Reflect on what makes you unique and valuable. Embrace your strengths and the qualities that make you who you are. Celebrate these aspects of yourself regularly.

Engage in Activities You Enjoy: Find hobbies and activities that bring you joy and fulfillment. Engaging in these activities can boost your mood and reinforce the idea that you are capable and worthy of happiness on your own terms.

Mindfulness and Meditation: Practice mindfulness and meditation to stay grounded in the present moment. These practices can help you connect with your inner self and cultivate a sense of inner peace and self-acceptance.

Pick one or two strategies that resonate with you and integrate them into your daily routine. For instance, you might begin by writing down three things you appreciate about yourself each day or setting a personal goal that excites you. As you practice self-validation, you'll likely notice a shift in how you perceive yourself and others. You'll feel more grounded and secure in your own worth, and this will naturally lead to healthier, more fulfilling relationships.

Narcissistic Patterns in Romantic Relationship

Interrupting Conversations

- Scenario: During a discussion, you notice that you often interrupt your partner to share your own experiences or opinions.
- Recognition: Reflect on these moments and consider how it might make your partner feel unheard and undervalued.

Seeking Constant Admiration

- Scenario: You frequently find yourself needing compliments or praise from your partner and feel upset if they don't provide it.
- Recognition: Acknowledge this need and consider how it might pressure your partner and strain the relationship.

Criticizing or Belittling

- Scenario: You catch yourself making negative comments about your partner's achievements or abilities.
- Recognition: Understand that these comments can damage your partner's self-esteem and the overall relationship dynamic.

Ignoring Your Partner's Needs

- Scenario: Your partner expresses a need for more emotional support or quality time, and you realize you've been dismissing these requests.
- Recognition: Recognize that fulfilling your partner's needs is essential for a balanced and healthy relationship.

Here are some strategies to help identify these harmful patterns

We've identified that we might have some... let's call them 'quirks' in our relationship behavior. Now what? Well, it's time to do some serious self-investigation.

First up: self-reflection. Looking inward isn't exactly our forte but it has to be done. Take the time to consider your interactions with your partner. Think about moments when they seemed upset or withdrawn and ask yourself if your actions or words could have contributed to their feelings. At the end of each day, take five minutes to think about your interactions with your partner. Start a journal. I know it sounds a bit 'dear diary,' but can be incredibly helpful. Writing down your conversations and conflicts can reveal patterns that you might miss in the moment.

Next up: listen to feedback. And I mean really listen, not just waiting for your turn to defend yourself. If your partner says they're feeling undervalued or criticized, resist the urge to dismiss it. Instead, take a deep breath and say, 'I hear you. Can you tell me more about that?'. And don't just stop at your partner. Ask your friends or family for their honest opinions about your relationship behavior. I remember when I did this - let's just say it was a humbling experience. But, was it eye-opening!

Now, here's something that might feel a bit scary: professional help. The idea of spilling your guts to a stranger can feel pretty vulnerable. But let me tell you, seeing a therapist was one of the best decisions I ever made for myself and my relationship!!!!!

A good therapist is like a personal trainer for your emotional muscles. They can help you spot those blind spots you didn't even know you had. Doing couples therapy can also be a great option. A neutral third party can help mediate conversations and highlight harmful patterns.

Lastly, mindfulness. I used to think this was all about sitting cross-legged and saying 'om.' Turns out, it's actually about being aware of your thoughts, feelings, and behaviors in the moment. This awareness can help you recognize when you are acting defensively or seeking validation.

Here's a simple mindfulness exercise: Next time you're in a conversation with your partner, pay attention to your body. Are your fists clenched? Is your jaw tight? These can be signs that you're getting defensive. Take a deep breath and try to relax those areas.

So, here's your mission, should you choose to accept it: Pick one of these strategies and commit to trying it for a week. Maybe start with the journal, or ask a friend for some honest feedback. Whatever you choose, stick with it. This isn't about becoming a whole new person overnight. It's about making small, consistent changes that add up to big improvements in your relationships.

Building a Strong Foundation

We're talking trust, respect, and communication so open you could drive a truck through it.

I know, the idea of being an open book might make you break out in hives. But sharing your hopes, dreams, and yes, even your fears, isn't a sign of weakness. It's like giving your partner a map to your heart. And that's way more attractive than any facade we could put up. The first time I really opened up to my partner, it felt like standing naked in Times Square. But instead of judgment, I got understanding. Instead of rejection, I got acceptance. It was like she finally saw the real me and didn't run screaming for the hills.

We've got to move beyond our favorite topic (ourselves) and start genuinely considering our partner's needs and feelings. It feels like we're becoming a supporting actor but instead, we actually become the hero of our relationship story.

So how do we do this? Well, it's a process and includes several factors. We've already covered the basics like self-awareness, empathy, and active listening. Those are crucial, no doubt, but let's not rehash old ground. Instead, let's explore some new-ish concepts that can really take your relationship game to the next level.

Prioritizing Your Partner's Needs. That tricky give-and-take dance where both partners' needs matter is essential and might involve making sacrifices or compromises, which can be difficult but necessary for a balanced, healthy relationship.

For example, your partner's having a week from hell at work. They're stressed, they're overwhelmed, and they need support. Meanwhile, you've got tickets to this amazing concert you've been looking forward to for months. What do you do? The old you might have said, 'Tough luck, babe. I'm sure you'll figure it out!' and headed off to rock out. But the new, relationship-savvy you? You say, 'Hey, how about I cancel my plans and we have a quiet night in? You look like you could use some support.'

It might feel like you're sacrificing a kidney at first. But when you start prioritizing your partner's needs, they start doing the same for you. Suddenly, you're not just two people sharing a life, you're a team.

Genuine Consideration in Decision-Making. When making decisions that affect both of you, involve your partner in the process. Ask for their input and consider their preferences and concerns. For instance, if you're planning a vacation, instead of announcing, 'We're going camping, pack your bear spray,' try this: 'I've been thinking about a vacation. What kind of trip would you enjoy?' Then - and this is the crucial part - actually listen to their answer. Discuss potential destinations together and find a place that you both will enjoy. It might feel like you're giving up control but you gain a partner who feels respected and a relationship built on mutual consideration...which is worth way more than always getting your way.

Building Emotional Support. Showing emotional support is like being your partner's personal cheerleader, therapist, and comfort blanket all rolled into one. It means to be there for your partner in times of need, offering comfort, encouragement, and understanding when they face challenges.

Imagine your partner is going through a difficult time at work, feeling overwhelmed by deadlines and office politics. Instead of dismissing their concerns or making the conversation about yourself, focus on their experience. You might say, "I can see that work has been really stressful for you lately. It sounds like you have a lot on your plate. Is there anything I can do to help or any way I can support you through this?" This shows that you are not only listening but also willing to be a source of comfort and support.

Offering encouragement is another crucial aspect of emotional support. Suppose your partner is preparing for an important presentation and feels anxious about it. Rather than brushing off their anxiety, acknowledge their feelings and provide positive reinforcement. You could say, "I know you're nervous about the presentation, but I believe in your abilities. You've put in a lot of hard work, and I'm confident that you'll do great. I'm here for you no matter what." This type of encouragement can boost their confidence and show that you are invested in their success.

Understanding is also vital in providing emotional support. If your partner experiences a personal loss, such as the death of a loved one, your role is to offer a compassionate ear and a shoulder to cry on. You might say, "I'm so sorry for your loss. I can't imagine how hard this must be for you. Please know that I'm here to listen whenever you need to talk, and I'm here to support you through this." This empathetic response demonstrates that you are sensitive to their pain and willing to share in their emotional burden.

The tricky part for us narcissistic types: this isn't a one-way street. You've got to let your partner support you too. This mutual exchange builds a balanced and healthy relationship. I know, vulnerability isn't exactly our strong suit. But next time you're stressed, try saying, 'Work's been kicking my butt lately. I could really use your support'. By being open about your needs, you show vulnerability, which can deepen the emotional connection between you two.

Practicing Patience and Understanding. Relationships take patience, especially when you're dealing with arguments or misunderstandings. It is like trying to eat soup with a fork. It's frustrating, it takes forever, and you'll probably want to flip the table more than once. But it is the secret sauce that can turn your relationship around. Try to be patient by giving your partner room to fully express themselves. Don't jump to conclusions or get defensive right away. Instead, approach conflicts with an open mind, trying to understand where they're coming from and find some middle ground.

Consistency in Actions. You know that feeling when someone makes a promise, and you're thinking, 'Yeah, right. I'll believe it when I see it'? Well, guess what? You've probably been the promise-breaker more times than you'd care to admit.

The thing is that building trust is like trying to build a castle with toothpicks. It takes forever, it's frustratingly delicate, and one wrong move can send the whole thing tumbling down. But when you get it right? It's a thing of beauty.

Consistency isn't exactly our strong suit as recovering narcissists. We're more about the grand gestures, the big promises, the 'I'm going to change everything starting right now!'

declarations. But here's a little secret I've learned the hard way: it's the small, everyday actions that really count.

Let me tell you a story. I once promised my partner I'd be more attentive. I made a whole speech about it, complete with dramatic hand gestures. I felt pretty good about myself. Fast forward to the next day, when they're trying to tell me about their work problems, and I'm half-listening while scrolling through my phone. Not exactly 'Partner of the Year' material, right?

That's when it hit me: trust isn't built on promises. It's built on follow-through. It's about aligning your actions with your words, day in and day out. It's showing up, even when it's not convenient or exciting.

So, how do we do this? Start small. If you say you're going to call, call. If you promise to help with the dishes, roll up those sleeves and get scrubbing. It might not feel glamorous, but it's relationship gold.

This consistency thing? It's tough. There will be days when you just don't feel like it. Days when you'd rather focus on yourself. That's okay. Acknowledge those feelings, then do it anyway. There will be slip-ups along the way, and that's fine. The key is to keep trying, keep showing up, keep aligning your actions with your words.

Pick one area where you want to build trust. Maybe it's being more attentive, or helping out more around the house, or simply following through on your commitments. Now, commit to being consistent in that area for the next month. No excuses, no 'I forgot,' no 'I was too busy.'

It might feel boring at times. You might feel like you're not getting enough credit. But stick with it. The view from a relationship built on trust is pretty spectacular.

Shared Values and Goals

Shared values and goals are the bedrock of any strong relationship. They're like a compass that helps both partners navigate life's journey together. For example, if both partners value family and have a goal of starting one, it creates a bond that strengthens the relationship.

I get how this concept can be a real challenge to grasp and implement. You're probably used to focusing primarily on your own needs and goals. The idea of genuinely considering someone else's aspirations might feel foreign, maybe even threatening. But learning to do this can be incredibly transformative, not just for your relationships, but for your personal growth too.

Think about it this way: a relationship isn't a one-person show. It's a partnership, a dance between two individuals with their own dreams, fears, and hopes. When you start to see your relationship this way, it opens up a whole new world of connection and understanding.

Now, I know this shift doesn't happen overnight. It takes practice and patience. But there are some strategies you can use to start moving in this direction:

Self-Reflection: Before you can understand your partner's values and goals, you need to be clear about your own. Take some time to really think about what matters to you. What are your core values? What do you want to achieve in life? This self-awareness is the first step in being able to relate to and understand others.

Open Dialogue: Once you're clear about your own values and goals, it's time to have an open, honest conversation with your partner about theirs. This isn't about judging or criticizing. It's about listening and trying to understand. Ask questions like, "What's most important to you in life?" or "What are your dreams for the future?" Then really listen to their answers.

Find Common Ground: As you discuss your values and goals, look for areas of overlap. Maybe you both value financial security, or you both dream of traveling the world. These shared aspirations can become the foundation of your relationship.

Embrace Differences: It's unlikely that you and your partner will align on everything - and that's okay. The key is to respect and support each other's individual goals, even if they're different from your own. If your partner dreams of starting their own business, for example, think about how you can support that dream, even if it's not your personal goal.

Compromise and Flexibility: Sometimes, your goals might conflict with your partner's. This is where compromise comes in. Be willing to adjust your plans or find creative solutions that work for both of you. Remember, it's not about winning or losing - it's about finding a way forward together.

Regular Check-ins: Values and goals can change over time. Make it a habit to regularly discuss your aspirations and how you're both working towards them. This keeps you connected and on the same page.

Celebrate Each Other's Successes: When your partner achieves a goal, celebrate it as if it were your own. This reinforces the idea that you're a team, working together towards shared success.

Seek Professional Help: If you're really struggling to shift from a self-centered perspective, don't hesitate to seek help from a therapist or relationship counselor. They can provide strategies tailored to your specific situation.

As you learn to genuinely consider your partner's needs and goals, you'll likely find your relationship becoming stronger and more fulfilling. You might even discover aspects of yourself that you never knew existed. And as you practice empathy and compromise, you're developing skills that will serve you well in all areas of life.

Practicing Respect in Daily Interactions

Respecting each other means listening to each other, valuing each other's opinions, and treating each other with kindness. It might involve actively working to curb tendencies to dominate conversations or dismiss your partner's feelings. Small acts of respect in daily interactions can make a big difference. For instance, showing appreciation for your partner's efforts, being considerate of their feelings, and supporting their decisions can enhance mutual respect. Learning to practice genuine respect can be transformative. It's not just about following rules or going through the motions - it's about fundamentally shifting our perspective and behaviors.

Here's how you can make respect a daily practice:

Active Listening: Make a conscious effort to listen to your partner without interrupting, without dominating the conversation, and without thinking about your next point. Instead, next time your partner is talking, focus entirely on what they're saying. Don't interrupt, don't plan your response. Just listen. You might be surprised at what you learn when you truly tune in.

Showing Appreciation: It's easy to take our partners for granted, especially when we're focused on our own needs. But try making a habit of noticing and acknowledging your partner's efforts, big or small. Did they handle a difficult situation well? Thank them. Did they remember something important to you? Let them know you noticed. These small acknowledgments can make a big difference.

Being Considerate: This one requires us to step outside of our own perspective. Consider your partner's feelings and needs when making decisions. If you know your partner's had a rough day, how can you support them? Maybe it's taking on some extra chores or just giving them space to decompress. The key is to tune into their needs, not just your own.

Supporting Decisions: Show that you trust and support your partner's decisions. Even when they differ from what you would choose, show that you respect their judgment. It's not about always agreeing, but about trusting your partner's ability to make choices for themselves.

Avoiding Dismissiveness: It's easy to brush off our partner's concerns or feelings, especially if we don't understand them. Instead of saying, "You're overreacting," try to understand why they feel the way they do. This opens up dialogue and shows that you value their perspective.

Sharing Space in Conversations: Sharing space in conversations is about balance. If you find yourself monopolizing discussions, make a conscious effort to step back and invite your partner's input. Ask for their thoughts, their opinions. Show that you value what they have to say.

Apologizing When Necessary: Apologizing when we're wrong can be tough, especially if we're used to always needing to be right. But a sincere apology can be incredibly powerful. It shows humility, accountability, and respect for your partner's feelings.

Encouraging Growth: Supporting your partner's growth demonstrates that you see them as an individual with their own aspirations, not just an extension of yourself. Celebrate their achievements, and support their goals, even if they're different from your own.

As you incorporate these practices into your daily life, you might find that not only does your relationship improve, but you start to feel different too. You might discover a sense of fulfillment in supporting your partner's happiness. You might find that by respecting others, you gain a deeper respect for yourself. Who knows?!

Understanding Each Other's Perspectives

Understanding your partner's perspective involves empathy and active listening. It requires us to step outside of our own viewpoint and truly try to see the world through someone else's eyes. The good news is that you have to master one thing only: make a conscious effort to listen without immediately thinking of how it affects you or preparing your response. Can you do that?

Let's break this down into practical steps:

1. Try to feel what your partner is feeling. Next time your partner expresses sadness or frustration, try to imagine yourself in their shoes. Instead of dismissing their feelings or trying to fix the problem, simply acknowledge what they're going through. Instead of saying, "You'll get over it," try, "I can see that you're really upset. I'm here for you."

2. After your partner shares something, try paraphrasing what they've said. This serves two purposes: it shows that you're really listening, and it gives your partner a chance to clarify if you've misunderstood. For example, "So what I'm hearing is that you felt ignored during the meeting, and that made you really frustrated. Is that right?"

3. Hold back from making judgments or jumping to conclusions about what your partner is saying. Give them the space to express themselves fully before you respond. Remember, understanding doesn't mean you have to agree with everything they say. It's about respecting their right to their own perspective.

4. Be present in the moment, fully engaged in the conversation. Put away distractions like your phone or the TV, and give your partner your full attention. Show through your body language (make eye contact, nod to show you're listening, lean in slightly) that you're truly present and engaged.

5. It is a great way to deepen your understanding. If something isn't clear, don't be afraid to ask for clarification. Questions like "Can you tell me more about that?" or "How did that make you feel?" show that you're genuinely interested in understanding their perspective.

6. Recognize that your partner is a separate individual with their own unique experiences and viewpoints. These differences don't have to be a source of conflict. Instead, they can be an opportunity for growth and learning. Try to approach these differences with curiosity rather than judgment.

7. Be patient with yourself and your partner. Developing empathy and understanding is a skill, and like any skill, it takes practice. There will be times when you slip back into old patterns, and that's okay. What matters is that you keep trying. Developing the habit of understanding and empathy takes time, especially if it's not your natural tendency.

Expressing Love and Affection

Regularly expressing love and affection is obviously essential for creating a deep bond with your partner. It might require you to make a conscious effort to move beyond self-centered tendencies and genuinely show appreciation and care for your partner.

You've probably heard of the "Five Love Languages" concept by Dr. Gary Chapman. These love languages provide a framework for understanding how different people express and receive love. It's a game-changer when it comes to understanding how to show love in a way that really resonates with your partner. The key here is to figure out what makes your partner feel truly loved and appreciated.

Now, you might be thinking, "How am I supposed to know what their love language is?" Well, here's a radical idea—just ask them. I know, it sounds simple, but it's often the most direct route to understanding.

Once you've got a handle on your partner's love language, you can start tailoring your expressions of love to what really speaks to them. It's like learning a new language, but instead of words, you're learning how to communicate love in a way that your partner truly understands and feels.

Let's break down these love languages and look at some practical ways to put them into action:

Verbal Affirmations: This is all about expressing love through words. If this is your partner's language, try starting their day with something like, "I feel really lucky to have you in my life because you're so supportive." It's a simple statement, but it can have a profound impact.

Physical Touch: This isn't just about sex—it's about those everyday moments of connection. A hug when they get home, holding hands while you watch TV, a kiss on the cheek as you pass each other in the kitchen. These small touches can speak volumes. Physical touch is a powerful way to show affection and includes holding hands, hugging, kissing, or even a gentle touch on the arm. Physical touch can convey love and reassurance, making your partner feel cherished and valued.

Thoughtful Actions: This might involve doing something special for your partner, like cooking their favorite meal, taking care of a chore they usually do, or planning a surprise date night. It's about showing that you're paying attention to their needs and wants.

Quality Time: It is all about giving your partner your undivided attention. Put away the phones, turn off the TV, and really focus on each other. This could be as simple as taking a walk together or having a deep conversation over coffee.

Small Gestures: These are the little things that show you're thinking of your partner throughout the day. Leave a sweet note in their lunch box, send a loving text, or pick up their favorite snack on your way home.

Nurturing the Relationship

It isn't a one-and-done deal—it's an ongoing process that requires consistent effort and attention. But trust me, it's worth every ounce of energy you put into it. It's about consistently showing up for each other, supporting each other's individuality, respecting boundaries, and cheering each other on. The payoff? A strong, healthy, and fulfilling relationship.

Here's how to do it:

Quality Time: This is about more than just existing in the same space. It's about actively engaging with each other. Maybe you cook a meal together, take a walk in the park, or binge-watch that new series you've both been dying to see. Making an effort to engage in shared activities shows your partner that you value them and your time together. It's a powerful way to deepen your connection.

Maintaining Individuality: This might sound counterintuitive, but while togetherness is important, maintaining individuality is equally crucial. Supporting your partner's individuality doesn't mean you're any less important. In fact, it strengthens your bond. Encourage each other's personal interests and hobbies. Maybe your partner loves painting while you're into rock climbing. That's great! These individual pursuits allow you both to grow as people, which in turn enriches your relationship.

Balancing Togetherness & Personal Space: It is a delicate dance, especially if you're used to wanting constant attention or control. But respect for each other's need for alone time is vital. It prevents that suffocating feeling that can creep into relationships and keeps things fresh. Remember, missing each other a little can be good for your relationship.

Encouraging Each Other's Growth: Supporting your partner's goals and celebrating their achievements doesn't diminish you—it enhances your relationship. When your partner succeeds, you succeed too. Their growth contributes to the growth of your relationship as a whole.

Overcoming Common Challenges

Life has a way of throwing curveballs at us, doesn't it? And when you're in a relationship, those challenges can really put your bond to the test. But navigating these bumps together can actually make your relationship stronger. Let's talk about how to tackle some common challenges as a team.

Dealing with External Stressors: We're talking work pressure, money worries, health issues—you name it. These things can creep into your relationship and stir up tension if you're not careful. The key here is open communication. If work's got you stressed, don't bottle it up. Talk to your partner about what's going on. Let them in on what's swirling around in your head. And remember, support is a two-way street. If your partner's drowning in deadlines, maybe you can pick up some extra chores around the house. It's not about solving their problems, it's about showing them you've got their back. When it comes to tackling big issues, like financial stress, approach it as a team. Sit down together, crunch the numbers, and brainstorm solutions. Two heads are better than one, right?

Impact of External Stress on Relationships: External stress can make anyone cranky or withdrawn. If your partner's not quite themselves, try to be patient. Give them some space if they need it. And hey, if you've had a rough day, resist the urge to take it out on your partner. Instead, explain how you're feeling and why. It's about supporting each other, not finding someone to blame.

Coping Strategies for External Challenges: Coping with stress can make anyone irritable or distant. If your partner's not acting like themselves, try to be patient and understanding. Give them space if they need it. When you've had a rough day, communicate your feelings instead of lashing out. Supporting each other through tough times is crucial.

Navigating Life Transitions Together: Whether you're moving, changing jobs, or starting a family, these changes can be both exciting and scary. The key is to face them together. Talk about your hopes and fears. Plan together. Celebrate the wins and work through the challenges as a team. For example, if you're moving to a new city, discuss your excitement and fears about the new place. And when your partner is going through a big change, be their cheerleader. Listen to their worries and offer encouragement. If they land that big promotion, celebrate it! And if they're struggling, roll up your sleeves and help out however you can.

Strategies for Maintaining Relationship Stability: To keep your relationship stable long-term, consistency is key. Regular check-ins, addressing issues as they come up, and continuously nurturing your bond—these are the building blocks of a lasting relationship.

CONCLUSION

Congratulations on reaching the last pages! Your commitment to reading this entire book speaks volumes about your dedication. You have demonstrated the courage to silence your ego and confront each page with an open mind and heart. I am profoundly grateful for your trust in this process and your openness to change.

This book marks only the beginning of your path to overcoming narcissistic behaviors and building healthier, more fulfilling relationships. While the tools and strategies provided here are invaluable, continued progress often requires additional support. If it is within your means, I strongly encourage you to find a therapist who can provide personalized guidance and help you delve deeper into your journey of self-discovery and healing. A professional can offer the expertise and support necessary to navigate complex emotions and behaviors.

Additionally, consider joining a support group where you can connect with others who are on similar journeys. Sharing experiences and learning from others is crucial for sustaining long-term change; it offers encouragement and accountability, making the path to transformation less daunting.

Never give up on your journey. It is not a linear path; it requires habits, consistency, and an unwavering commitment to improvement. Embrace the process, be patient with yourself, and celebrate your progress along the way. Remember, change is a marathon, not a sprint. With habits, consistency, and a solid support system, you can achieve lasting transformation and enjoy the rewards of a more fulfilling and authentic life.

Building new habits and maintaining consistency are fundamental aspects of this journey. Think of habits as the building blocks of your new self. Establish a routine that includes daily reflection, mindfulness exercises, and positive affirmations. Over time, these practices will become second nature, reinforcing your commitment to change and helping you maintain a healthier mindset.

Understanding what drives you is crucial for sustaining your journey. Motivators can be internal, such as a desire for self-improvement and emotional stability, or external, like improving relationships with loved ones. Identifying these motivators provides a clear sense of purpose and direction. Reflect on what truly inspires you. Is it the prospect of healthier, more fulfilling relationships? Or perhaps it's the internal peace that comes from self-acceptance and a reduced need for external validation? Whatever your reasons, keep them at the forefront of your mind to fuel your determination.

Staying motivated also requires perseverance and adaptability. Tracking your progress is essential to stay motivated and recognize how far you've come. Regularly reflect on your achievements and areas needing improvement; journaling can be a powerful tool for this purpose, allowing you to document your journey, celebrate successes, and learn from setbacks. Set aside time each week to review your progress. Ask yourself what worked well, what challenges you faced, and how you overcame them. This reflection not only highlights your growth but also reinforces your commitment to continuous improvement.

Here are some techniques to help you stay focused, especially during challenging times:

First, try setting realistic goals. I used to set these crazy, over-the-top goals because I thought that's what successful people did. But all it did was set me up for disappointment. Now, I break things down into smaller, doable steps. Breaking down larger goals into smaller, achievable steps can make a big difference. For example, if your larger goal is to build more meaningful relationships, start by making a conscious effort to listen more actively during conversations with friends or family. Set a goal to have one meaningful, distraction-free conversation each day.

Celebrate each milestone along the way. After a week of successful, engaged conversations, reward yourself with something enjoyable, like a favorite treat or a relaxing activity. This way, you're acknowledging your progress and keeping your motivation high. As you continue, gradually increase your goals. Maybe next, you aim to express appreciation more often or work on being more empathetic. Each small, achievable step contributes to your larger goal of improving relationships, and celebrating these steps keeps you encouraged and committed to your journey.

Another great technique is to visualize success. I used to think this was New Age nonsense, but every morning, I take a few minutes to picture what it looks like to achieve my goals. It's like a mental rehearsal, and it keeps me motivated throughout the day. This practice can reinforce your commitment and give you a mental boost when you need it most. It's also important to stay flexible. Sometimes a particular strategy might not work as well as you hoped. If that happens, don't get discouraged. Be open to trying different approaches until you find what works best for you.

Finally, seek inspiration. Surround yourself with uplifting content. Read books, watch videos, or listen to podcasts that inspire and motivate you. These can provide valuable insights and keep your spirits high during tough times.

As you move forward, keep in mind that setbacks are a natural part of any journey. Don't be discouraged by them. Instead, view them as learning opportunities that can guide you toward better understanding and managing your traits. The key is consistency and resilience. Stay motivated by remembering why you started this journey and the positive changes you aim to achieve. Relapses into old behaviors can be discouraging, but they are also opportunities to learn and grow. Understanding that setbacks are part of the process will help you manage them with resilience. When a setback occurs, take a step back and assess what triggered it. Was it a stressful situation, a particular relationship dynamic, or perhaps an internal conflict? By identifying the cause, you can develop strategies to handle similar situations better in the future. Developing strategies to manage relapses can prevent them from derailing your progress. Create a relapse prevention plan that includes identifying situations, emotions, or people that trigger old behaviors and developing healthy ways to cope with triggers, such as mindfulness exercises, talking to a trusted friend, or engaging in a relaxing activity.

Never give up on yourself! Each day is a new opportunity to make different choices, to be kinder to yourself and others, and to move closer to the person you aspire to be. Keep pushing forward, stay committed, and remember that every effort you make is a step towards a brighter, more compassionate future.

BONUS TOOLS

Transform Your Interactions and Self-Awareness with Our Exclusive Bonuses

When you purchase "Stop Narcissistic Behaviors," you don't just receive a book—you gain access to powerful tools that deliver real, observable changes. Our "Trigger Tracker," "Personal Growth Blueprint," and "Family Dynamics Workbook" are designed not just to inform you, but to transform you:

BONUS 1: Family Dynamics Workbook: Specifically designed for those raised by narcissistic parents, this workbook helps you understand and heal from the unique challenges of your upbringing. It includes guided exercises to identify and address past traumas, develop self-compassion, and reconstruct a healthier self-image.

BONUS 2: Trigger Tracker: Experience fewer outbursts and maintain better control over your emotions by identifying your personal triggers. This tool helps you recognize the early signs of distress and manage them effectively, leading to smoother, more positive interactions in both personal and professional settings.

BONUS 3: Personal Growth Blueprint: See measurable improvements in your relationships within just four weeks. This structured program guides you through daily actions and reflections, helping you to build healthier relationships, enhance empathy, and develop a deeper understanding of yourself and others.

With these tools, you're not just learning about narcissistic behaviors—you're actively reshaping them into healthier patterns.

Your path to a clearer, more fulfilled life is just a Qr-code away!

MORE HEALING BOOKS FROM US

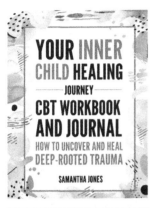

Your Inner Child Healing Journey

How to Uncover and Heal Deep-Rooted Trauma. A CBT Workbook and Journal to Face Abandonament, Neglet and Abuse, Improve Self-Esteem & Regain Emotional Freedom

Samantha Jones

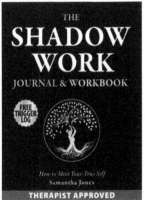

The Shadow Work Journal & Workbook

How to Meet Your True Self: Integrate & Transcend Your Dark Side through Self-Discovery Exercises. Deep Guided Prompts for Inner Child Soothing, Healing & Growth

Samantha Jones

Self Love Workbook

A Guided Journey with Life-Changing Activities & Self-Care Rituals to Truly Fell in Love with Yourself. Heal Emotional Wounds, Recognize Your Worth & Embrace Your Uniqueness

Frida Elowen

Made in the USA
Columbia, SC
25 September 2024

43001771R00063